CULTURE SHOCK!

Israel

Dick Winter

Graphic Arts Center Publishing Company
Portland, Oregon

In the same series

Australia	*Italy*	*South Africa*
Borneo	*Japan*	*Spain*
Britain	*Korea*	*Sri Lanka*
Burma	*Malaysia*	*Syria*
Canada	*Morocco*	*Taiwan*
China	*Nepal*	*Thailand*
France	*Norway*	*USA*
Hong Kong	*Pakistan*	*Vietnam*
India	*Philippines*	
Indonesia	*Singapore*	

Illustrations by Shirley Eu
Cover photographs from Life File Photographic Library by
Terry O'Brien and Christine Osborne
Photographs by Digi Dekel unless otherwise noted

© 1992 Times Editions Pte Ltd
Reprinted 1994, 1995

This book is published by special
arrangement with Times Editions Pte Ltd
Times Centre, 1 New Industrial Road, Singapore 1953
International Standard Book Number 1-55868-088-8
Library of Congress Catalog Number 91-077244
Graphic Arts Center Publishing Company
P.O. Box 10306 • Portland, Oregon 97210 • (503) 226-2402

Printed in Singapore

To my mother and father,
for their support;
and to Israel,
for my life.

TARSUS

ANTIOCH

ALEPPO

HAMATH

THE
GREAT
SEA

BYBLOS

DAMASCUS

SIDON

TYRE

PTOLEMAIS

CAPERNAUM

GALILEE

CAESAREA

SAMARIA

JOPPA

JERUSALEM

GAZA

JUDEA

SALT
SEA

Seu.

ISRAEL

C 46AD

CONTENTS

Drivers on the highway stop to pay a moment of respect on Holocaust Memorial Day in Israel. (Photo by Vered Peer, IPPA Ltd)

Journey about Zion, and go around about her:
count her towers, citadels, and fortresses.
Consider her palaces.
Set your heart on her strength:
that you may tell it to the generations to come.

—Psalms 48: 12–13

"You don't have to be crazy to be a Zionist, but it helps."
—Chaim Weizmann,
first president of Israel.

SYRIA

LEBANON

Mediterranean Sea

Sea of Galilee

Haifa•
    Nazareth•

ISRAEL

Tel Aviv-Jaffa •
Holon •
Rehovot •
    Jerusalem•
Ashdod •
   Bethlehem•

Gaza •
    Dead Sea

Beersheba •

JORDAN

EGYPT

Eilat
Gulf of Aqaba

    Israeli-occupied territories

FOREWORD

This book is not only about Israel and its relatively well-known history and politics, but about the far more enigmatic Israelis who dwell in those harder-to-find grey areas which are so characteristic of the Middle East. Explaining just who they are, how they behave, and exactly what makes them tick is one of the main purposes of *Culture Shock! Israel*. But above all, it's about what it's like to live here, and to participate in the unforgettable experience of its daily life.

Living in Israel is like stepping back in time. And this is not only because of the country's incredible history, which seems to come alive in Jerusalem's Old City walls, the Crusader fortresses of the Galilee, and the more contemporary war memorials that are in virtually every town and village.

Israel is one of the few places on earth where geography *is* history, whether it be the land where Jesus Christ and King David lived, or the modern battlefields which have made it the focus of more attention than any country in the world. Here, the ground seems charged, from the epic sagas chronicled in the Bible more than 2,000 years ago, to the dramatic headline-making events of the present day.

But for Israel, stepping back into the past refers to the very special Israeli personality. Israelis seem to live in a far simpler time, before aspirations of independence and statehood could be taken for granted, and the idealism which accompanied them became cynically outmoded.

An anachronistic nation, Israel continues to hold on to what could be called the World War II mentality – a mindset characterized by patriotism and simpler, more fundamental values. Indeed the most sorely missed emotion of that long gone, naive time still lives on; the feeling that, to put it simply, everyone is together.

Israeli life is permeated by an intensity and dynamism found in few other countries, precisely because national survival is not taken for granted. Israelis remain powerfully, intensively, and passionately involved in their politics, their culture, and their religion.

Apathy, the great neurosis of the post-World War II era, is virtually nonexistent, for the very simple reason that Israelis are too busy trying to hold on to their emotions to give it much thought. And the analogy to World War II has sometimes been dangerously clear. During the Gulf War, the country seemed to evoke memories of London during the 1940 blitz, and the Scud missiles which fell on Tel Aviv brought to mind for many the V-2 rocket bombs of the Nazis.

When the air raid sirens were sounded, and "watching the sky" once again became a popular – and dangerous – national pastime, feelings of national solidarity were magnified to unprecedented proportions, and the near euphoric defiance with which the Israeli people faced the missiles of Saddam Hussein won them international admiration.

Those same air raid sirens continue to be heard twice a year, marking the nation's two memorial days. The sirens sound in honor of not only those who died in Israel's many wars, but in memory of the 6 million who perished in the Holocaust, thereby bringing the country together physically, emotionally, spiritually.

But Israel is above all a land of stark contrasts. The old with the new, the secular with the religious, the Jew with the Arab. One of the most striking features of the country is its singular newness; the newness of the people (many of them immigrants), the language, the culture, music, art, literature, theater, and even of the troubled and often stormy national politics.

Physically, so much in Israel is so new that when traveling on

Statue of the man who started it all – Theodore Herzl, the founder of Zionism.

roads which traverse the great desert wilderness, whole cities seem to appear on the horizon as if by some miracle.

Yet with all the building and settlements so characteristic of a new nation, one cannot help but notice how much of the land still remains vacant. These vast open spaces are the most concrete manifestation of Israel's youth, exemplified by the fact that the state has yet to celebrate its 50th birthday.

All this is contrasted greatly by Israel's overpowering history. Wherever one goes, from the Southern Negev Desert to the Northern Galilee Panhandle, there seems to be – in the air, like the dust of ages – the overriding feeling of ancientness. Even for the secular, the stones scattered all over the hills of Jerusalem seem to be not only ancient but holy.

So it's only fitting that as far back as 1902 Theodore Herzl, author of *A Jewish State* and the founder of Zionism, entitled his novel of the Zionist dream *Altneuland*, or in German, "Old Land-New Land."

This is *Culture Shock! Israel.*

Chapter One

A LAND OF IMMIGRANTS

"Israel will be open to Jewish immigration and the ingathering of exiles; it will foster the development of the country for the benefit of all its inhabitants; it will be based on freedom, justice and peace as envisaged by the prophets of Israel; it will ensure complete equality of social and political rights to all its inhabitants irrespective of religion, race or sex ..."

—The 1948 Israeli Declaration of Independence.

IN THE BEGINNING

As late as 1989, 41 years after the creation of the state of Israel and more than 100 years after the first wave of immigrants began arriving, official statistics revealed that as much as half the total Jewish population of the country was born somewhere else.

A look at the nation's leadership (both past and present) tells a similar story: David Ben-Gurion, Israel's first prime minister, was born in Russia and spoke Hebrew with a distinctive Russian accent; Golda Meir, though also born in Russia but emigrated to the United States at the age of 8, spoke with a grating American accent; Menachem Begin and Yitzhak Shamir were born in Poland and still speak with a pronounced Polish-Yiddish accent; and Israel's president at the time of writing, Chaim Herzog, was born in Ireland and speaks with an unforgettable Irish brogue.

In fact, one of the unique items mentioned in the biographies of national leaders like Yitzhak Rabin, Moshe Dayan and Ariel Sharon is not that they spent their formative years abroad, but that, on the contrary, they claim the prestigious distinction of having been born in Israel.

Different Languages

It's amazing how many different languages you will hear while walking down the average street in Israel. Yiddish, French, Spanish, English, German, Amharic (the language of Ethiopian Jews), Hebrew, Arabic, and in recent years especially Russian. Even Israel Radio broadcasts in 12 different languages. Day to day life is full of surprising encounters which emphasize this polyglot aspect of the Israeli character.

Once, while standing in line at a grocery store, I couldn't help but notice that the woman at the cash register spoke a different language to each customer. English with one, Spanish with the other, and Hebrew the next.

I couldn't resist asking her where she had learned such good

The next generation of Israelis – black and white editions. These Israeli schoolchildren are going on a field trip.

English. With a smile, she replied that she was born in India. English was her second language; but Hindi was her first!

"But where, for the love of God, does the Spanish come from?" I asked.

"Oh," she answered nonchalantly, "my husband's Argentinean."

Is this your typical grocery store check-out girl? Welcome to Israel!

THE IMMIGRANTS

The first Zionist immigrants who settled in Israel in 1882 were Russians, so it's somehow fitting that 100 years later, history should come full circle with today's massive wave of Russian immigration from the Soviet Union. Some 1 million Russian Jews are expected to immigrate to Israel by 1995. That would be 1 million people out of a total population of only 5 million. The impact this would have, and is already having, on every facet of life in the country – from politics and the economy to the social order – is incredible.

But the history of the state of Israel, both before and after its establishment, has been marked by just such sporadic immigrant waves, each causing a corresponding shake-up in the existing society of the day. Every *aliyah* (meaning "to go up" in Hebrew; also referring to periods of mass Jewish immigration) became the central event of their time in Israel.

The Ingathering of Exiles

Israeli history can be categorized less by dates than by immigrant waves: the pioneering Russians and East Europeans who fled anti-Semitism in the early part of this century; the Germans who fled Nazi Germany in the 1930s; the North Africans who sought freedom from Arab oppression in the 1950s; and finally, today's Soviet Jews, who are again fleeing anti-Semitism and economic hardship. Immigration is the foundation of Israel, its *raison d'être* and the cardinal principle of its existence.

One of the most crucial documents in Israeli history was the infamous White Paper of 1939, a British policy which led to the closing off of Palestine to Jewish immigration. With millions of Jews trapped in Nazi-occupied Europe and barred by the British government from immigrating, the Jews of Palestine were radicalized, and began a struggle against Britain which led to guerrilla warfare and eventually to independence.

In the 1948 Israeli Declaration of Independence, which in the absence of a formal written constitution represents the fundamental basis of Israel's law and ideology, the very first sentence about the future policies of the state declares that "Israel will be open to Jewish immigration and the ingathering (return) of exiles."

One of the most important Israeli laws, The Law of Return, is an expression of this very same principle. Simple but revolutionary, it grants Jews anywhere in the world the right to immigrate to Israel and to receive Israeli citizenship.

THE RUSSIANS

The Russian *aliyah*, the most current expression of these ideological foundations, has turned present-day Israel into an even more exciting place than usual. In Tel Aviv, Jerusalem, Haifa, Beersheba, Tiberius, and even in the small developing towns on the borders, Russians seem to be springing up everywhere – young and old, fair and dark, cosmopolitan Muscovites and Leningraders along with their more rural brethren from Gruzia and Azerbaijan.

Signs and advertisements in Russian have begun to appear in stores and buses, and they are as big a surprise to the Israelis as they are to the visitors. On the streets, one hears Russian, Russian, and more Russian. And when asking passers-by for the time, it seems like there is a 50 percent chance that they will reply in Russian. And when you signal incomprehension and tap your wrist repeatedly to explain, they will understand and with a sad smile show you their watch.

Such an unprecedented flood of immigrants in a country as small as Israel has caused great problems. Seemingly insurmountable shortages of housing and jobs, along with soaring welfare costs, threaten to ruin an already overburdened economy.

But with it all, it is still a great pleasure for Israelis to welcome these Russian Jews, and especially their children. These children represent the future, and the country is like a proud new parent – full of joy at having a baby, despite the knowledge that life will be full of sleepless nights, diapers, and worry. A national effort has been required to cope with the crisis, and Israel with its many wars is well accustomed to national efforts.

The daily attempt to pitch in expresses itself in many ways. I once helped a young Russian who had difficulty buying a particular drink from a small cold drinks stand. The owner of the drinks stand couldn't understand her repeated requests for "Pepsi, Pepsi." With some difficulty, I explained to her, mostly with the use of hand signals and the word "nyet," that there was no Pepsi in Israel, but one can request Coke instead. If I had been able to speak Russian, I would have added the reasons – political rather than economical – which have kept Pepsi from being sold here. Afterward, I told the perplexed kiosk owner just what that mysterious Pepsi was.

THE ETHIOPIANS

The case of Ethiopian Jews provides an even more striking example of just how important immigration is to Israel. In the spring of 1991, as the nation was already staggering under the weight of 110,000 Russian Jews who had arrived in the first half of the year, with immigrant absorption centers filled to capacity and shortages in housing and employment already reaching critical proportions, Israel carried out Operation Solomon. In 30 hours, using numerous air force and civilian planes, 14,500 Ethiopian Jews were airlifted into the country, only hours before Ethiopia's capital, Addis Ababa, fell to rebel forces. If these Jews had not been rescued, they would have met with an unknown (and perhaps unthinkable) fate.

The basic question of where to put them all – many were eventually housed in hotels – faded into the background as Israelis joyfully celebrated the fact that the last of the Ethiopian Jews had finally made it home. Seven years before, in Operation Moses, 7,000 Ethiopian Jews were rescued. But since then, the Ethiopian government had adamantly refused to allow those remaining behind to emigrate.

Such rescue operations – and there have been many in Israeli history – emphasized above all that the supreme consideration is always the "open gate." Social and educational difficulties, housing shortages and unemployment, wars and uncertainty all become irrelevant in the face of this one overriding factor.

I remember how during Operation Solomon, when Israel Television interrupted its regular telecast to broadcast the live coverage of the ongoing airlift, my usually stoic neighbor came running out of his house to tell me the news.

"But how will we deal with them all?" I asked.

His answer revealed much about the Israeli view of immigration. With a downward wave of his hand at the irrelevancy of the question, he said, "that's another problem entirely."

On television and radio that night, several politicians provided the sad historical footnote to the successful rescue operation by linking it to a topic never far from the Israeli mind: the Holocaust. If Israel had come into existence sooner, when the world had closed its gates to European Jews, perhaps the 6 million who were murdered by the Nazis could have been rescued too.

The successful absorption of the Ethiopian Jews of Operation Solomon has been made much easier by the fact that they have been helped considerably by their predecessors from Operation Moses. This has involved not only explaining the ins and outs of Israeli life, but also the ins and outs of modern life. Many Ethiopian Jews, for instance, had never seen a faucet with running water until they came to Israel – a real example of culture shock.

But old immigrants helping new ones, the veterans coming to the aid of the newcomers, has been an invariable part of every single one of Israel's immigrant waves. All in all, the massive influx of Ethiopian Jews has given a unique face to the already diverse Israeli immigrant mix. Not brown-skinned like many African-Americans, but virtually jet black, the Ethiopians add much to the already colorful Israeli scene. Israel, with its intimations of "the East" and "the West," now can claim a touch of "the South" too.

Ethiopian Jews always bring to mind for me the seemingly non sequitur of the United Nations' "Zionism Equals Racism" resolution. In most parts of the world, racism is associated with the color of one's skin. So how, I wonder, would those who voted for this 1975 condemnation of Israel respond to Operations Moses and Solomon? They would, of course, deny that Israel has provided the world with a shining example of the irrelevancy of color.

For Israelis, the question of the skin color of Ethiopian Jews hasn't been a problem. In the 1950s, they had already gotten used to the fact that many of the Moroccan Jews are quite dark (not to mention the Yemenites, who are even darker). In the rainbow scale of Israeli color, the Ethiopians are but one more shade.

FATHERS AND SONS

Israel is one of the easiest countries in the world where you can be a stranger. One thing you won't find here is xenophobia (the fear or hatred of foreigners), for the simple reason that most of the country seems to be made up of them! Nobody turns around and stares when a foreign language is spoken; there are already so many different accents that one more is hardly even noticeable.

There are literally no strange sights on the Israeli streets. The whole world is represented, including the Far East, because during the late 1970s, Israel took in a relatively large number of Vietnamese boat people.

The Old World Israeli: an Iranian newspaper vendor.

"Fathers and Sons" refers to the Israeli phenomenon of immigration and the melting pot of races. The parents, who emigrated from some foreign land, still speak their native language at home (despite having long ago mastered Hebrew), and in many cases insist on retaining the culture and mentality of their birthplace. This is the "old world Israel" – whether it be the Yemenite Jews who still begin the day by eating a raw clove of garlic (whew!), or the German Jews who are still addicted to the classical music of Beethoven and Bach, or the Moroccan Jews who still enjoy the traditional singing and folk dancing of Arabic North Africa.

Old and New

One of the best examples of these old world roots is Israeli cuisine, which rather than indigenous is actually a combination of ethnic dishes from all over the world. Every home seems to offer its own menu, depending on where the family emigrated from: *gefilte* fish is still a first course for those who came from Europe; for North Africans, the great delicacy is *couscous* (a kind of specially prepared fine flour); and for Jews who made their way to Israel from Kurdistan, the treat is *kube* – an extremely tasty meat soup.

And then there's the children, who look, act, and sound totally different. They are no longer German, Moroccan, Yemenite, Russian, or Ethiopian Jews, but instead simply just Israelis. This is the "new Israel," and exactly what this means the remaining chapters of this book will describe.

But one of the most striking characteristics of the country is the contrast between these two generations, and the bridge between them. It often comes as quite a surprise to hear these typical Israelis suddenly speak to their parents in some foreign language at home, and a moment later break back into their native Hebrew, which of course does not have the faintest trace of any foreign accent.

In this sense, Israel resembles the United States, which has its own version of the melting pot, Emma Lazarus ("Give me your

Israeli fathers and sons going into the desert to see the promised land.

tired, your poor"), and the American Dream. The difference is that in Israel this phenomenon is relevant not only to a minority of the citizenry, but to almost everyone – for Israelis having immigrant parents is not the exception but the rule. And Israel adds its own special touch to the melting pot ethic.

One of the legendary Israeli myths (which many claim to be true) is that immigrant Jewish couples, who to their great misfortune are "physically unattractive" (ugly is the word), happily discover that the children they have in Israel, despite all the laws of heredity and genetics, somehow turn out to be incredibly beautiful. The magical-mystical influence of the land of Israel is said to work wonders!

THE ISRAELI ARABS

One of the great ironies of the Jewish state is that approximately 18 percent of its citizens are not Jewish. Of these, the vast majority – some 14 percent – are Moslems, and the remainder are Christian, Druze, and Circassian. Moslem as well as Christian Arabs who live in Israel (and not in the Occupied Territories) are collectively known as "Israeli Arabs." In short, they are a study in contrasts.

At first glance, their story is a positive one: citizens, voters, and office holders, they are well represented in the Knesset, Israel's parliament, and are full-fledged members of political parties and trade unions. Large numbers of Israeli Arabs live together with their fellow Jews in the Tel Aviv twin city of Jaffa, in Haifa, Acre, and Ramle. A visit to Nazareth, the largest Israeli Arab city, shows just how much this minority has prospered in the years since Israel became a state. The large number of Israeli Arabs enrolled in the country's universities is yet another example of their progress.

With economic modernization has come social change: a large percentage of Israeli Arabs have abandoned traditional agriculture to become professionals and urban workers. In terms of local politics, Israeli Arabs have benefited from the influence of the country's

An Arab coffee vendor, carrying his container of drink in East Jerusalem.

democracy. A generation ago, all of the Arab leadership was hereditary, with the control in the hands of village elders and clan chieftains (the *mukhtars*). Today, Israeli Arabs rule their own towns and villages by means of democratically elected governing councils.

The Arab Dilemma

But a closer look shows that despite all the progress and democratization, Israeli Arabs are caught in a dilemma. Promised in Israel's Declaration of Independence equal rights together with religious and cultural freedom, the one thing they are not promised is an Arab national home.

In an identity crisis worthy of the best psychologists, the Israeli Arabs are trapped right in the center of the Middle East conflict. As Arabs, they can easily identify with the surrounding states that are Arab national homes – all of which, except Egypt, remain in a state of war with Israel. As Palestinians, they have only to look to the Territories and their Palestinian inhabitants, who are under military occupation, to find themselves in another problematic identity crisis. As Israelis, they can easily see the Arab states as military threats, and the Palestinians in the Territories as enemies hostile to the state.

This dilemma, and the question of divided loyalties which accompanies it, is brought into the open in one very practical way – Israeli Arabs are among the few citizens of the country not drafted into the army. The small number who do serve in the Israel Defense Forces are volunteers.

As if the multiple identity crisis of Israeli Arabs wasn't enough, they have also found themselves coping with the fundamental problem that as a minority, like minorities the world over, they are discriminated against by the majority in power.

Despite increased educational and political opportunities, Israeli Arabs feel, and justifiably so, that they have not been given their rightful piece of the economic pie. For example, on the surface, the beautiful city of Haifa – Israel's San Francisco on the Mediterranean – seems to be a place of ideal Jewish-Arab coexistence; Arabs and Jews living together in peace and harmony. In Haifa, one only has to visit the city's "Bet Gefen" (House of the Vine), a center for Jewish-Arab understanding, to come away with a favorable impression. But a closer examination reveals that many of Haifa's Israeli Arabs hold lower-class jobs; they are the builders, the manual laborers, and the taxi drivers.

Minorities have similar complaints in most countries of the world, but the problem in Israel is compounded by the fact that the nation is still in a state of war with various Arab states, and with the majority of the Palestinian people. When the explosive emotions of the Middle East are suddenly brought to the surface by a terrorist attack or even by war, the sensitive relationship between Israel's Jews and Arabs can become very tense.

The dilemma of the Israeli Arabs is clearly revealed in national politics. Until recently, they were great supporters of the Israeli left – the Labor Party, the Socialist Party, the Citizens Rights Movement, and especially the Israeli Communist Party. However, with the decline and fall of communism worldwide, and with the ongoing Middle East conflict, more and more Israeli Arabs have abandoned the left. And they are turning back to a disturbing direction – religious fundamentalism.

Today, one of the most powerful Arab politicians, the mayor of Nazareth, is the leader of a movement which represents the new wave on the Israeli Arab political scene: the Islamic fundamentalist party.

THE BEDOUINS

One of the most interesting of Israel's many ethnic minorities are the Bedouins. Part of a group of nomadic Arab tribes scattered across the deserts of the Middle East, the Israeli Bedouins live mostly in the Southern Negev desert. There, alongside the desert

An Israeli Bedouin.

flatlands and dunes which make up most of the countryside, many of their tents and herds can be seen.

Living mostly off camel, goat, and sheep herding, the Bedouins are also known the world over as great traders – and as great hosts. To be their dining guest is an unforgettable privilege: lamb, rice, and a return to the centuries-old tradition in which the status of guest and host still has great meaning.

But perhaps the most remarkable thing about the Israeli Bedouins is not their renown as great hosts, but rather their fame for something entirely different: they are known as the best trackers in the world. Yes, trackers – the same sort of trackers you see in old Cowboy and Indian movies. Such a long-forgotten trade has not only found its uses in Israel, but has become one of the most important occupations in the land.

The Bedouins are among those few Israeli Arabs who volunteer to serve in the army, and as trackers they are included in the units which guard Israel's borders. When a terrorist infiltration is detected and an alert is sounded, the Bedouin trackers find themselves in a crucial, and dangerous, job.

I once accompanied a Bedouin tracker who, during the night in rough terrain and with only a flashlight, was able to track down a terrorist who had managed to penetrate into Israel. He was also able to tell if the terrorist had been running, and whether he or she was carrying any equipment.

Later, in a more relaxed moment, I asked the Bedouin just how he was able to do this. Looking at me as if I had asked a truly dumb question, equivalent to asking a fish how it swims, he shrugged and simply said, "I see."

THE DRUZE

The most fascinating Israeli minority is without doubt the Druze. This is not only because of the splendid looks and dress of the Druze men (huge bushy moustaches along with a white headdress, a kind of black bloomers, and cummerbund), but due to the simple fact that they are a mystery. Although they speak Arabic, the Druze are not Moslems but the descendants of a sect which has its roots in Egypt some 900 years ago.

Living in the remote, isolated mountainous areas of Syria, Lebanon and Israel, the Druze have for centuries managed to preserve their traditions and customs. Most importantly – and here lies the fascination – they have somehow succeeded in keeping their religion a complete secret. Known in general as a combination of Judaism, Islam, Christianity, and Sufism, the particulars of the Druze religion have been passed down through generations, and are known only to the faithful and their priests. It is remarkable that even in this cynical day and age, none of them has "defected" to tell a curious world – and Israelis are the most curious of all – just what the Druze religion is all about. One item, however, that has managed to leak out is that reincarnation somehow plays a part in the faith. The rest has remained a secret.

The Druze in Israel are much more of a success story than the Israeli Arabs. More successfully integrated into Israeli society and more fully accepted as Israelis, perhaps the key reason for this is that since the 1950s, they have been drafted into the army. Unlike Israel's Arabs, the Druze have throughout the years (and throughout the wars) paid for their citizenship with blood – which the average Israeli considers to be very significant indeed.

The most important soldier in my platoon of paratroopers was the one whose job was to fire the most crucial weapon in combat – the heavy machine-gun. And that soldier was a Druze. After all the dangers that the platoon went through, we knew that we had a comrade for life in our friend who just happened to be a Druze.

Another case in point: perhaps the most influential Druze in Israel today is not the mayor of a Druze village or a Druze Knesset member, but rather a journalist by the name of Rafik Halavi. One of the chief editors of the most important television program in the country, Halavi edits the nightly Hebrew news on Israel Television.

The Druze are for the most part free of the dilemma of conflicting identities which plagues Israeli Arabs. Most of their problems are caused by geography rather than ethnicity. They have always lived in Galilee, which is an undisputed part of the state. However, when the Golan Heights were conquered by Israel in 1967, another group of Druze became an issue – the Druze of the Golan.

Living literally on the Syrian border at the foot of Mount Hermon, these Druze villagers found themselves after 1967 under Israeli rather than Syrian military rule. After 1981, when the Golan Heights were annexed, they became formal citizens under Israeli law.

The Druze of the Golan believe that they are in a crossfire of the Israeli-Syrian dispute over the Heights, and that someday they are liable to find themselves under Syrian rule again. Thus, despite having received Israeli citizenship, most of them have refused to vote; and unlike the Druze in Galilee, they are not drafted into the army.

But in contrast to the Arabs in the Territories, the Druze of the Golan Heights are not openly hostile to Israel, and it is perfectly safe, and even recommended, to visit them. During winters, their mountainside villages are the only ones in the country which are covered with snow.

Outside the largest Druze village on the Golan, Migdal Shams ("the Tower of the Sun" is the Arabic translation), is located one of the oddest tourist attractions in the world: the Hill of Shouts. Here, using loudspeakers, megaphones, and sometimes only their own strained voices, Druze from across the border in Syria stand on a hill and shout messages to their relatives in Israel.

Making for one of the strangest scenes on the planet, you can see (and hear) these two groups of people, so close yet so far away, shouting to each other across the border between two countries still in a state of war.

THE CIRCASSIANS

If the Druze are the most fascinating ethnic minority in Israel, then the Circassians are certainly the strangest.

The Circassians are Moslems, but they are not Arabs. Their origins are not in the Middle East but in Russia, of all places. When the Ottoman Empire stretched its northern frontiers into what are now the Moslem republics of the Soviet Union, one of the peoples they converted to Islam were the inhabitants of the Kokaz Mountain region. When the Russians conquered the area in 1864 and attempted to re-convert these people to Christianity, the Circassians left their homeland and migrated to Syria, Jordan, Iraq and Israel in order to preserve their faith.

The Circassians, concentrated mostly in two villages in the lower Galilee, remain to this day a living anomaly. Though they speak their native language – Circassian – as Moslems they also speak Arabic. Yet they do not look in any way like Arabs, but rather like Russians or East Europeans. The strangeness of their history somewhat resembles that of another small ethnic minority in Israel – the Armenian Christians who live in one small quarter of Jerusalem's Old City.

The Circassians made headlines in recent years because of one of the most famous Supreme Court cases in Israeli history. A Circassian by the name of Izzat Nafsu, an officer in the Israeli Army who had been convicted of espionage, was exonerated by the court and set free in a dramatic trial which rocked the country.

As an Israel Radio reporter, I covered the case and recalled how, shortly before the verdict was announced, hundreds of Circassians crowded the small Supreme Court building to show support for their native son.

"How can you be so sure," I asked one of the villagers at the time, "that Nafsu is innocent?"

The old Circassian, his face seamed by years of hard work, looked at me with a slight smile and simply answered, "Because he's a Circassian."

Such a response, with its accompanying logic, could have been given by any one of Israel's many ethnic minorities, or indeed by the country's ethnic majority.

WHO CAME FIRST?

There's no better way to conclude this chapter on Israel's people than with the most famous comedy sketch in Israeli entertainment history: a variation on Abbot and Costello's *Who's on First?* It can best be called "Who came first?" Two of the best known Israeli entertainers, Arik Einstein and Uri Zohar, put this sketch on film in the 1970s and since then it has become legendary.

The skit begins with the two performers dressed in traditional garb as Arabs, standing on a deserted beach around the turn of the century, watching a ship come into port.

There, taking part in the first wave of Jewish immigration to Israel, are two Russians (by film magic, once again, Einstein and Zohar – but this time dressed as Russian peasants) celebrating their arrival, kissing the ground and singing Hebrew songs in thick Russian accents.

Observing this display, one of the Arabs asks the other, with the classic indifference which is the mark of the slower pace of village life, just who these strange people are. The other Arab pauses and then simply answers: "Jews." And the way he sadly moans out the Arabic word for Jew – "Yee-huud" – seems to hilariously express all the troubles to come for the Arabs.

The next scene shows the two Russians, now standing on the beach in place of the Arabs, looking toward the port. They are looking at two German Jews (once again Einstein and Zohar, this time dressed as immaculately meticulous Germans, in shirts and ties) celebrating their arrival, and talking excitedly with thick German accents.

The Russians, now "veteran Israelis," look on this display with

barely disguised contempt, shaking their heads with stern disapproval and saying to each other in their thick Russian accents, "Who
do these people think they are, professor this and professor that,
with their *gefilte* fish and classical music?"

And so the pattern of the sketch is established. Next come the
North Africans, singing and dancing in their Arabic garb. This time,
the Germans are on the beach, looking on in anger, shaking their
heads in dismay, talking with their heavy German accents about the
nerve of these strange newcomers, and asking with outrage, "Where
were they when we built the country, made the desert bloom,
established the state, and fought the wars?" And on and on, with
each new wave and ethnic group repeating the invariable pattern.

Here then, in this sketch, is *Culture Shock! Israel* in a nutshell –
Israeli history, the Israeli personality, the Israeli mentality, and
above all, a classic example of Israeli humor.

Chapter Two

RELIGION IN ISRAEL

Shabbas! Shabbas!!*

" * sabbath, sabbath. "

"The three principal objectives of Judaism are: (1) the fostering of the unity of … universal Israel; (2) the perpetuation of Jewish tradition; and (3) the cultivation of Jewish scholarship. Given agreement on these three, the rest can take care of itself."

—Isadore Epstein, *Judaism.*

THE MEN IN BLACK

It could well happen on the flight over on your way to Israel. Sitting in the seat next to you is one of the stranger sights you have thus far managed to encounter in this life: a vision in black. Black felt hat (or maybe it's mink), black long coat, some kind of black vest with all sorts of strange white frilly things streaming out of it, and other assorted layers below that – all this despite it being summer and quite warm.

The apparel looks to be something out of the 17th century, possibly even the 16th, but the countenance seems to come straight from Mars – odd gaps amid sideburns and a beard, and strangest of all, springing out from the area around the ears are extremely long, curly "sidelocks" (a word that until now was not a part of your vocabulary).

Twice during the flight, this apparition joins several other similar types at the back of the plane and engages in what looks like praying. And never have you seen it done with quite such intensity, with everybody fervently chanting, swaying, and rocking back and forth. What is this? *Culture Shock! Israel*? Well, not exactly, because most Israelis also join you in not knowing exactly what this is.

Hassidism

The strangest and most extreme corner of the religious scene in Israel, the textbook explanation is that these Jews, known as ultraorthodox or "Hassidic" (the word means "righteous or pious" in Hebrew), dress this way because the leaders of their particular sect did so 200 years or so ago in Eastern Europe. The sidelocks and frilly white things are the results of Biblical injunctions which indeed can be found somewhere in the Old Testament.

But beyond this technical explanation, which doesn't help you in the least to explain exactly why it's so important for them to dress and look this way, it remains as much a mystery to 99 percent of the Israelis as it will be to you. I myself have studied the works of

Martin Buber, who is sometimes called the father of Hassidism, and although he was an otherwise great philosopher, I have never quite managed to figure out his connection with the sidelocks.

The Land of the Living Bible

Perhaps it would have been far more appropriate to open this chapter with a more powerful scene. While walking inside the walls of Jerusalem's Old City, you suddenly hear the bells tolling in the church which marks the site where Christ was crucified. And at virtually the same time, the loudspeakers of the Moslem mosques begin broadcasting in Arabic the beautiful, often chilling call to prayer. All this while you are gazing at the holiest site in Judaism – the surviving Western Wall of the Temple, destroyed some 2,000 years ago. It's simply a great thrill to be a Christian, a Moslem, or a Jew in the country which is the focus of these three major religions, and it is a feeling powerful enough to be felt by the rest of the world's remaining religionists.

Practicing your faith in Israel is an experience never to be forgotten. The Dome of the Rock is a mosque so beautiful that one can almost imagine Mohammed on his white stallion ascending to heaven from it, and on some days the Sea of Galilee shimmers so smooth and blue that you yourself might be tempted to try a walk on the water.

It is a cliché to call Israel the land of the Living Bible, but when you drive your car through the lower Galilee on the road from Mount Tabor to the Sea of Galilee, you will actually wonder at the long distance Jesus walked – a feeling you might have missed out on when originally reading that particular verse in the Bible. Not to mention the personal sense of awe that I experienced during a night army march when, at one point, I reached exhaustion and it seemed like the end of the world to me. To make matters worse, I was stunned when told that we were now located in, of all places, the Valley of Armageddon!

Islam and Judaism, so close yet so far. Pictured here are the holy places of the two faiths – the Western Wall and the Dome of the Rock.

A Land of Great Emotion

Israel is more than anything else a land of great emotion, and even the most cynical person can't help but sometimes find himself or herself caught for a moment and touched.

For me, it happened on my second day in Israel, a Friday afternoon, when I was strolling around the emptying streets of Jerusalem. (At that time, I didn't yet understand why they were emptying.) I saw an elderly, bearded ultraorthodox Jew striding up the middle of the street, ringing a bell and, like the town criers of old, joyfully proclaiming, blazoning, trumpeting: "Shabbas! Shabbas!"

I knew no Hebrew upon arriving in Israel, but that little bit of Yiddish ("Sabbath! Sabbath!") I did recognize. As strange as his getup seemed to me, I could not help but be moved by the intensity, the religiousness, the simple love of God that seemed to permeate the scene.

A Fact of Life

But religion in Israel is more than anything else a fact of life which influences every aspect of day-to-day existence in the country. Want to go out and see a movie Friday night? If you don't live in the Tel Aviv or Haifa areas, forget about it. The theaters are closed, and there is no public transportation if you don't have a car.

Were you used to doing your shopping and errands on Saturday? Well, in Israel, get unused to it. Aside from some few and far in-between exceptions, there is nothing open; Saturday is the day of rest, and God apparently does not consider shopping to be a restful enough activity.

And that terrific Chinese or Mexican restaurant which you finally found with some effort? Well, the next time you go there and see a big sign that reads "We are now kosher" hanging in the window, you can forget about your favorite dish of sweet and sour pork.

And in the Mexican restaurant, that great beef enchilada which you were so fond of will, instead of melted cheese, now be covered with some unrecognizable goo; about the only thing you can be sure of is that there are no cheese, milk, or dairy products in it.

On the other hand, in how many countries in the world can you take your kids on a morning walk right down the middle of the biggest highway in the city with no risk whatsoever of being run over? In Israel, on the Yom Kippur holiday, not only can you but thousands of people do it.

However, it is regarding the matter of time – the structure of the week, the day, and indeed of the entire year – that religion in Israel is most strongly felt. As periods of time were set down in the Old Testament of the Bible, so they exist to this day in Israel, and this takes some getting used to.

The week begins on Sunday, which is simply called "the first day" in Hebrew. Israel could well be the only country in the world where business – including banking – is conducted as usual on that day. And for possibly the first time in your life, you will begin to be consciously aware of when it is sundown. On Fridays or the eve of holidays, if you don't buy your food a few hours before sundown, you'll discover that the stores are closed, and will find yourself facing a 24-hour fast you had no intention of carrying out.

A Unique Israeli Phenomenon

Friday afternoons are in fact a uniquely Israeli phenomenon, with everybody frantically running from store to store stocking up on so much food that you would think they were getting ready to hibernate for the winter instead of merely preparing for the weekly 24-hour vacation. But if you did manage to get all your shopping and other errands done, then when the sun goes down and the sirens go off to signal the beginning of the Sabbath, like the average Israeli, you will sit back, take a deep breath and say to yourself, "I made it through another week. Shabbat Shalom!"

In case you haven't noticed, or haven't yet done the simple mathematics of subtracting the sum number of rest days from the total number of work days in a 7-day week, then here comes the bad news: Yes, most people in Israel work a 6-day week. Not much good news there, but I can offer a bit of consolation. When you get used to the new routine, you will find that time flies by amazingly fast, and one of the negative aspects of that long remembered weekend – getting depressed on the last night at the prospect of facing the new week ahead – simply does not exist in Israel. There's not enough time for it!

As far as the Biblical concept of the year is concerned, in Israel the new year begins not in January but in September. Not that Israelis don't celebrate on the night of December 31 with big parties – they do (for some reason they call the night the Sylvester in Israel, and I haven't yet discovered why) – but the entire orientation of the year turns around September, when the New Year holiday, or Rosh Hashana as it is known, usually falls. Around that time, not only do schools and universities begin anew after the long summer vacation, as they do in other countries, but the new calendars come out, and the television, newspapers and radio bombard you with year-end summaries, retrospectives, and soul-searching. Before long, with everybody wishing you "Happy New Year," making plans, and talking about their new year resolution to quit smoking for good this time, autumn will begin to have that beginning-of-the-year feeling for you as well.

THE RELIGIOUS ISRAELI

Contrary to what you might have thought, the majority of Israel's citizens are not religious. Only about 20 percent of the population are what Israelis themselves define as "observant Jews." I'll leave the complicated and touchy question of definitions to somebody else (a long explanation you might well endure several times during your stay here and not come out very much more enlightened).

41

However, in Israel the definition is made very simple indeed: a male who wears a skullcap – a small, round, usually knitted head covering which is worn to obey the Old Testament injunction "to cover thy head in the sight of God" – is considered to be a religious Jew. For women, the story is different and far more complicated, which makes the job of discerning whether they are observant or not much more difficult. But for males, at least the skullcap greatly simplifies things.

So there is no need for long explanations about the differences between Orthodox, Conservative, or Reform Judaism, though these divisions do of course exist in the country. (And the relatively few members of Israel's Conservative and Reform branches will no doubt want to skin me alive for this generalization.) In any event, this head covering, or *kipa* as it is called in Hebrew, is the symbol of the religious Jew in the same way the strange garb and sidelocks of the ultraorthodox symbolize Hassidic Judaism.

When Robert F. Kennedy's assassin, Sirhan Sirhan (who was born in East Jerusalem), was asked why he chose to kill the senator when at that time all the American presidential candidates were equally pro-Israel, he answered that he had seen Kennedy on television during a campaign visit to a Los Angeles synagogue wearing a *kipa*. It was a fatal association which changed the course of modern American history. In Israel, you will soon get used to what in every other country on the planet would be considered a strange sight: men and boys with the *kipa* on their heads.

Coping with the Sabbath

But aside from the head covering, there are of course many other customs which mark the religious Israeli. The Old Testament injunction "to observe the Sabbath" means, among other things, that from sundown Friday until sundown Saturday – the exact times of which are published in all of the country's newspapers – you can forget about phoning that friend or crucial business contact who happens to be religious, because it is forbidden for them to answer the phone. The prohibition on working or "violating the Sabbath" in any other way means no cooking, no radio or television, no cleaning, bathing, or showering. Even switching on the lights is considered taboo.

It is interesting how modern technology has helped the observant Jew cope with these rather difficult and harsh rules. The food is prepared before Friday sundown and kept warm by special electrical devices, and there are even automatic monitors that switch the lights on and off according to prearranged times, so that the religious don't have to ruin their eyesight by observing the age-old tradition of reading by candlelight.

And why can't this same automatically-run electricity be used to operate, say, a telephone answering machine so that you can at least receive a message? Nice try, but sorry. Telephone answering machines are also forbidden. Why, pray tell? Well, we have now reached, and rather quickly at that, the murky grey area which requires the judgment of an official rabbi from the Chief Rabbinate of Israel, whose job is to consult the ancient texts and try to find the connection between the Old Testament and telephone answering machines.

Silence was Golden

It was fascinating to see what happened during the Gulf War, when some 39 Scud missiles hit Israel, and the radio was vital for getting the 90-second warning, during which you had to run for your life into a sealed room, put on a gas mask, and wait for the broadcast of further instructions.

At first, the Chief Rabbinate announced in a special ruling that because it was a matter of life and death, turning on the radio for the religious would be allowed on the Sabbath. Then the rabbis ruled that since the very act of switching on the radio is forbidden, observant Jews should instead turn it on before the Sabbath, and leave it on, except they should put it in a closet so it won't be seen. Are you following me so far? Then – and this next development shows the power that the religious wield in the country – the Israel Broadcasting Authority announced that on every Sabbath during the war, one of the four radio stations in the country would be turned into "a silent station," which would broadcast only in the event of a missile attack. This way, the radio could be left on, but would emit no offensive, forbidden sounds except in the event of a life or death situation. Perhaps only a rabbinical mind could come up with such an ideal solution, no?

Well, now we come to the other side of the coin in the issue of religion in Israel. One of the stations that was blacked out during the war happened to be a very popular one called "The Voice of Music," which plays classical music at all hours with no commercial interruptions. So for an entire weekend, instead of Brahms, Mahler, and Aaron Copeland, classical music lovers got the soothing, tranquil, but somewhat boring sounds of utter silence. Was this fair? Well, welcome to Israel anyway!

Thank God it's not Friday

Another one of the major Sabbath injunctions is the prohibition against travel. Wherever a religious Israeli wants to spend the weekend, he or she must get there before Friday sundown.

I remember riding on a bus one Friday afternoon and noticing how one religious guy who had just got on kept glancing at his watch in what seemed like a mounting sense of panic, until he apparently reached a decision, stood up, and immediately disembarked. The last I saw him, he was frantically hitchhiking back in the direction he just came from. Whether he made it back home in time before sundown I'll never know.

There are many similar stories of religious Jews who, upon returning to Israel by air on a Friday afternoon a short time before sundown, have walked all the way home from Tel Aviv's Ben

Gurion Airport rather than violate the Sabbath. One can only hope that they did not live in Eilat in the far south, or else they would probably still be walking today.

Kosher Laws

However, the kosher laws, in contrast to the prohibitions which affect the religious Israeli alone, will influence you directly. If, for example, your favorite food is lobster tail, as it is mine, then your stay in Israel will involve a considerable sacrifice, at least on the part of your salivary glands.

In brief, the kosher laws forbid pork (as do Moslem laws), seafood, and the mixing of meat and dairy products. This means that in the home of a religious Israeli, not only are meat and cheese products never served at the same meal, but in every kitchen there are always two sets of dishes: one for meat, the other for dairy, and never must the two meet. In a kosher home, ice cream is never the dessert after a meal of chicken or beef; and you won't be pouring real milk in the coffee that finishes it all off. So, long-loved culinary habits take a beating in Israel. If you are dying to buy a ham and cheese sandwich for lunch, forget it – salami and cheese, maybe, but you must first purchase two separate sandwiches and then slap them together, hopefully out of the sight of any overtly religious types.

But not to worry. Most, if not all, of the "forbidden fruits" – shrimp, spare ribs, and even bacon – can be found in Israel. (Although to my infinite sadness, the one item I have not yet been able to locate is lobster tail. Israel is, unfortunately, the land of milk and honey, but not of lobster thermidor.)

There are still many restaurants – the Chinese ones are your best bet – that pride themselves on not being kosher. However, the trend seems to be going the other way. Even some Chinese restaurants have knocked the pork and shrimp dishes off their menus in the hope of regaining that lost religious clientele.

All public eating places, such as the average cafeteria at work, are kosher, as are most kiosks and cafes. It is only fair – is it not? – that at work, the religious Israeli should also be able to eat in the company cafeteria, even if this means a sacrifice on the part of his or her secular co-workers. Once again we have come to the heart of the issue of religion in Israel. For many, it's a thin line between simple consideration of others on one hand, and "religious coercion" on the other.

A Life of Prayer

But for the observant Jew, prohibitory injunctions and taboos are only one dimension of the religious life. Prayer is the backbone of any spiritual existence, and for them this includes morning and evening prayers, prayers before meals, prayers before going to bed, and indeed prayers for a myriad of other occasions.

During the basic training course of my stint in the paratroops, I remembered how incredibly pleased the entire platoon was that our sergeant was religious, because during his 10 minutes or so of prayer several times a day, we would all take a much needed rest. I swear, however, that despite the intensity of his prayers, he was still glaring at us from the corner of his eye, strewn as we were across the desert in various poses of blissful relaxation! Later during the Lebanon War, when we found ourselves in a particularly unfriendly town or village, we would take up defensive positions around this same sergeant, so that he could complete his daily prayers in peace.

THE ULTRAORTHODOX

The ultraorthodox in Israel are, to put it simply, a phenomenon. When you visit Jerusalem's Holocaust Memorial and Museum, which is called in Hebrew Yad VeShem ("A Place and a Name" – from a Biblical quotation from the book of Isaiah), you will see the famous photograph of a Nazi SS officer shearing the sidelocks from the head of a kneeling, terrorized ultraorthodox.

The ultraorthodox are a symbol – a symbol of faith and unremit-

Welcome to the closed world of Mea Shearim or "100 Gates." Note the "warning" sign at the top of the passageway's opening.

ting devotion which is one of the reasons why Judaism has managed to survive for over 2,000 years. But in Israel, they are also a source of controversy – ideological, political, and even economic tension.

The Beliefs

Believe it or not, many of these ultraorthodox do not believe in the state of Israel; this despite the fact that they not only live in the country, but hold substantial political and economic power. Having trouble following the contradiction? Don't worry, so do the vast majority of Israelis. In brief, the ultraorthodox doctrine teaches that the state of Israel can only arise after the coming of the Messiah. Since they believe that this has not yet happened, the establishment of the Jewish state is therefore considered to be a sin. Some leading ultraorthodox rabbis have even gone so far as to blame the Holocaust on this great crime; that Jews dared to embrace Zionism and believe in the creation of the Jewish state.

Another source of discord is the way in which the ultraorthodox live. Rather than spread out over the country and, in the words of the Zionist ideal, "work the land," they have instead for the most part recreated the East European ghettos once forced on them during centuries of persecution. The largest of these, Jerusalem's Mea Shearim ("100 Gates") neighborhood, is a must for every visitor. You will be fascinated by the high old walls and narrow passageways, not to mention the dress and looks of the neighborhood's Hassidic residents.

Above all, take note of the scores of signs and billboards, in Yiddish and English, many of them excoriating Zionism and the state of Israel, and others beseeching all visitors to "dress modestly," which in the ultraorthodox parlance means to cover up your bare arms and legs. In fact, except for the signs, you could just as well imagine yourself back in one of the 19th century Jewish ghettos of Warsaw or Minsk.

But for the average Israeli, there is something else about the ultraorthodox way of life which is even more irritating. The vast majority of them not only do not serve in the army (which for Israelis is a real sin), they do not work either. For thousands of ultraorthodox Jews, studying the Old Testament and other sacred texts is their sole occupation, with the *yeshiva*, or religious school, their solitary workplace. How then do they live, eat, rent or buy a home? In short, where does the money come from? The answer is the source of considerable anger within Israeli society. It is not from private donations, not from some higher institutional religious establishment, but from the hard-earned taxes of the average Israeli, secular as he or she may well be.

THE CONFLICT

Virtually all the major issues in Israel today revolve around either the question of the Territories (the Arab-Israeli conflict) or the religious question (the secular-religious conflict). Many remember with some fondness the calmer days before the Palestinian uprising and the Gulf War, when the controversy over a question as earth-shaking as opening the cinemas on Friday evenings caused an uproar big enough to make the headlines in all the country's newspapers.

Wars Between the Jews

An integral part of the platform of every political party in Israel is either "the battle against religious coercion," or "the fight to save the Sabbath," or even the middle ground compromise pledge "to preserve the status quo." And the rhetoric often gets hot and heavy, for it is well known that even without the wars against the Arab states, there are always the infamous, perpetual "wars between the Jews." And the term "status quo" is not a random one. Even before the formal establishment of the state of Israel in 1948, specific guidelines were set out to define the future relationship between the secular and religious in Israel.

The most famous of these was a 1947 letter written by the father of the country, David Ben-Gurion, who at the time was the leader of the Jewish settlement in the British mandate of Palestine.

"It is important to make clear," wrote Ben-Gurion, "that our purpose is not to establish a theocracy. In the future Jewish state, we shall also have non-Jewish citizens, and it is our obligation to guarantee their equal rights, and not to use coercion or to discriminate in religious or other matters."

However, later in this very same letter, Ben-Gurion goes on to declare that "it is clear the official day of rest will be on the Sabbath ... and all necessary steps will be taken to guarantee that any state kitchen for Jews will be kosher ... (we) will do all to satisfy the religious needs of the Orthodox, to prevent the division of the people." This 1947 document, known as the famous "Status Quo Letter," represents with all its apparent contradictions the beginning of a conflict which to this day is still not resolved.

Indeed, the religious issue goes to the heart of the question of just what kind of country Israel is. Not a theocracy but a democracy (except in the Territories, which are under military law), Israel is nevertheless a Jewish state. But even this definition causes problems because, according to Israel's 1948 Declaration of Independence, it will "maintain complete equality of social and political rights for all its citizens, without distinction of religion, race, or sex." Confused? If you are, then welcome to the conflict – you are well on your way to joining the ranks of the rest of the Israelis.

SOME TIPS ON RELIGION

- One thing that is guaranteed in Israel is freedom of worship, and tourist information centers in every city can help you find the place of worship of your choice. For

A crack in the Western Wall, filled with notes, prayers, wishes and requests.

special problems, Jerusalem's Tourist Information Center, or the Ministry of Religious Affairs, will take up the challenge and try to accommodate all faiths: Bahai's (one of their World Centers is in Haifa), Buddhists, Hindus, you name it. For Christians, directly inside the Old City's Jaffa Gate is the Christian Information Center, which can lend an immediate hand. For Moslems, "the Wakf," or Moslem Religious Authority, will gladly help.

- One of the most delightful customs in Judaism is to go to the Western Wall and place a small note in one of its many ancient crevices. Your wish is supposed to come true. Try it – it has worked two out of three times for me!

- For the adventuresome, spending a Friday evening Sabbath meal in an ultraorthodox home will be an experience you won't forget. This can be arranged through the tourist information centers, or at the Western Wall.

- Don't worry about the kosher laws if you happen to invite a religious Israeli into your home for a meal. Running around beforehand and separating all the dishes, or trying somehow to quickly conform to all the rules on the spot is a futile exercise. No one gets offended, and a simple phone call to your guest before the dinner inquiring about the problem will work everything out.

- A religious Jew in Israel will respond to the commonplace query "How are you?" not with the commonplace "Fine, thanks," or even with the less commonplace "Terrible," but with the Hebrew phrase "Baruch HaShem" (God be blessed). Not "Fine, God be blessed," or "Terrible, God be blessed," but the simple "Baruch HaShem." Don't be offended, even if it does sound like a non sequitur to you.

- In a synagogue, at the Western Wall, at the Yad VeShem Holocaust Memorial, or at funerals, men and boys are expected to wear a *kipa*, or in some manner cover their heads, out of respect. At Yad VeShem, at the Wall, and at most synagogues, head covering is provided for visitors. But if you unfortunately have to attend a funeral or memorial service, you must bring your own *kipa*. They can easily be purchased all over the country.
- When visiting a mosque, remove your shoes before entering. Do go and see the most fantastic and beautiful of them all, the Dome of the Rock, which is on the Temple Mount in the Old City, on the other side of the Western Wall. Visits are only allowed in the morning.

Chapter Three

POLITICS

"Zionism aspires to create a publicly guaranteed homeland for the Jewish people in the land of Israel."

—The Basel Program of the First Zionist Congress.

A PEOPLE OF POLITICS

Politics in Israel is like sex in other countries; those who are not doing it are either talking or thinking about it.

In Israel, everything is political, from the routine extradition of a wanted criminal to the prime minister's wife's fondness for shrimp dinners. Israeli governments have fallen not only over momentous questions of war and peace, but over issues as earthshaking as the landing of a jet plane after the onset of the Sabbath.

Israelis are obsessed, inundated by politics, whether it is the first five pages of the eight major dailies (not including, of course, the separate commentary sections), the hourly, half-hourly, and often minute-by-minute reporting on the radio, or even the hour-long nightly news programs on television (not to mention the myriad of interview shows and documentaries) – it's politics, politics, politics. I believe that a nuclear war somewhere in the world would only make page 6 of the Israeli papers, unless it happened to take place in the Middle East (which is, unfortunately, *not* a totally unlikely proposition).

On the Edge

But political life in Israel is much more than that. Israel is a country where politics are literally on the edge. Periods of political, economic, and social instability that occur in other developed countries about once a generation seem to rock Israel approximately every two months.

Whether it's the political earthquake of new elections, which can and often do occur at any time, or the economic shock of periods of high inflation, or the social upheavals that come with the absorption of a million new immigrants, Israel seems to jump from crisis to crisis. And that is only the internal instability; external threats have an even greater impact.

Diplomatic initiatives and pressures, tensions in the fragile United States-Israel relationship, ominous developments in the Arab states,

One of the smaller demonstrations. This group of Israelis want the Arab-Israeli dispute settled once and for all; their signs read "Yes to Peace" and "Stop the Occupation," in reference to the Israeli-occupied territories that include the Golan Heights and the Gaza Strip.

incessant Palestinian protests, sporadic terrorist attacks, not to mention *war* (or the attempt of a dictator like Saddam Hussein to, in his own words, "set fire to half the state of Israel") all send corresponding shock waves through Israeli politics. The resulting reassessments, realignments, and anguished soul-searching are almost weekly phenomenons.

An integral part of "politics on the edge" are the incumbent and omnipresent dangers. Israeli democracy is not only a relatively new experiment – less than 50 years old – but, with its massive internal and external pressures, is a fragile and often threatened institution.

The Knesset, Israel's parliament, includes several members who are located on the political spectrum somewhere in the neighborhood of Benito Mussolini, and there are also a few Israeli Communist parliamentarians who often seem on the verge of taking up the familiar call to drive Israel into the sea.

In short, Israeli politics, with all its excitement and emotion, could in no way be described as "entertaining." The threats to the very existence of the country's democracy are all too real and dangerous. The specter of fascism looms over the horizon, close enough to worry, if not frighten, every thinking Israeli.

But believe it or not, this is the great attraction of politics in Israel. Like many things in life, with the danger comes the interest, the excitement and the fascination. With all its instability, Israeli politics is above all alive, vibrant and dynamic. Apathy, along with American political terms like "personality politics," "non-issues," and the "silent majority," are concepts foreign to Israeli political life. Voter participation is among the highest in the world because the issues are all too real and dangerous. The majority is far from silent, and no one knows or cares much about the prime minister's sex life.

THE SYSTEM

There is a famous Israeli adage that goes like this: "Israel hasn't achieved victory in all its wars in spite of the mess, but because of it." This could also be said of the nation's politics, the only difference being that there is some doubt as to whether the final outcome is victory or defeat. What is certain is that the country's political life is a mess, the result of an institutional structure which has virtually proven its failure.

In the absence of a formally written constitution, much of Israeli democracy is based on government law. The election process is carried out through a proportional representation system – the 120 seats in the Knesset are allotted in direct ratio to the national vote. Thus the whole country is like one single legislative district, and most importantly, 1 percent of the vote is all you need to win a seat in the Knesset.

The Knesset

Voters cast their ballots not for specific candidates, but for party lists, which are determined by the parties themselves. The political party which receives the largest number of seats is given a chance to put together a majority government of at least 51 percent, which is equivalent to a minimum of 61 seats in the Knesset. The process of forming a government, known as "coalition building," lies at the heart of Israel's political dilemma.

According to Israeli law, it is the Knesset which holds supreme political authority in the country. In principle, it delegates power to the prime minister, and to the cabinet ministers whom he or she chooses, and a Knesset vote of no-confidence can just as easily take that power away. But in practice, it's the executive branch which really dominates the system. The prime minister, after putting together a coalition government with other political parties, parcels out the country's ministries (defense, foreign, finance, justice, education, etc.) and only then begins the real business of government.

As in most of today's modern democracies, a large group of inner advisers and "experts" (all of them non-elected) surround the

The center of Israeli political power: the prime minister's office.

prime minister, and it is this executive leadership which on the whole initiates political movement and change.

THE SPLIT

The systematic, institutional problems of Israeli politics are not so much a disease as a symptom. At the root of the problem is the 1 percent requirement needed to be elected into the Knesset. Because of this, small splinter and narrow-interest parties are able to win a place in the government, often finding themselves at the center of power. But their great influence derives not so much from the system, but from the circumstances which brought about a virtual split in Israeli political life.

This split has its beginnings in the 1967 Six Day War. Toward the end of that conflict, King Hussein of Jordan made the mistake of launching an attack on Israel. The Israeli Army, in a crushing victory, not only captured East Jerusalem and the Old City, but rolled victoriously all the way to the Jordanian border. The result: the conquest of what is now the Territories, a sizable area of land containing several large Arab population centers.

The Green Line Controversy

The Territories, which are currently under military occupation and law, are separated from the rest of Israel by an imaginary boundary known as "the Green Line." Existing only on maps (and deep in the national consciousness), the Green Line has been the most important line in Israeli politics ever since the Six Day War.

For 25 years, the debate has dominated Israeli political life: to keep the Territories or to give them back? In the decade after the war, the consensus, as expressed by the Labor governments of the time, was to return them in whole or in part, and in doing so exploit their value as a negotiating tool and bargaining chip. To paraphrase the famous United Nations Resolution 242, which was passed in the wake of the Six Day War, Israel should withdraw from the Territories in "a trade of land for peace."

But in 1977, a remarkable change took place. The election of the Likud government of Menachem Begin struck a new and revolutionary note: Israel should not only keep the Territories, but they indeed belong to her by Biblical right. These are not some nameless Israeli-occupied Arab lands but the Judea, Samaria and Gaza of the Hebrew Scriptures. "Greater Israel," as Begin called it, is a vast area which should be settled by Israelis and brought under Israeli law.

The great irony is that in 1978, this same Menachem Begin, who led the revolution against the principle of land for peace, made his mark in history by reaching a milestone peace agreement with Egyptian president Anwar Sadat precisely on the basis of this principle. Israel not only returned to Egypt the massive Sinai Peninsula, but uprooted the Jewish settlement which had been built there – in exchange for a peace that has since lasted nearly two decades.

However, despite the Egyptian-Israeli peace pact, the question of the Territories has not only remained at the center of national politics, but with the long-lasting Palestinian uprising and the continued controversy over the Jewish settlements, the debate has intensified. And more importantly, the country is now evenly divided over the issue.

The Knesset Kingmakers

This split is the most essential reality in Israeli political life today. It represents the real disease of Israeli politics, because it has turned what could be seen as the relatively small fire of the 1 percent election problem into a raging inferno.

When the nation was evenly divided in elections 49 percent versus 49 percent, the Knesset members that represented the remaining 2 percent found themselves in the enviable position of being made kingmakers. And these kingmakers have often been on the extreme fringe of Israeli political life.

A classic example was the infamous government crisis during

the spring and summer of 1990, when the situation reached the point of absurdity. At that time, the leaders of both major parties virtually promised the moon to the members of a few small parties in order to entice them (which is the nice way of putting it) to join their ranks, therefore swinging the delicate balance in their favor.

In a struggle that even Machiavelli would have called cynical, obscure and unknown Knesset members who represented only 1 percent of the Israeli citizenry were promised power over major government ministries; and instead of the all-important problem of the Territories, fringe issues such as who would get what political job, the passage of a law against the sale of pork, or the ban on billboards displaying models in swimsuits were given top priority as the leading policy questions of the day.

In the political intrigue that would have been extremely entertaining had it not been so sad, the contest veered dramatically back and forth between the Labor and Likud parties. A few ultraorthodox Knesset members even switched sides several times, all this on the orders of a rabbi who was not only anti-Zionist, but resided in Brooklyn, New York!

And above all, in a nation deep in economic distress because of gigantic defense costs and the prospect of absorbing hundreds of thousands of new immigrants, millions of dollars from public funds were doled out to these small parties in order to win their support.

The Israeli public viewed this entire roller coaster spectacle, which lasted several months, at first with excitement, and then with despair, and finally with disgust. Even Israel's president Chaim Herzog called it "a shameful episode," adding that "there must be a better way." Indeed, with all its political damage, perhaps the greatest harm was done to the country's moral code. The crisis seemed to prove the belief that when everybody steals, it is no longer theft, but "borrowing."

In the midst of the controversy, after the Labor Party of Shimon Peres barely failed to form a government, some 100,000 protesters demonstrated to demand election reform, and hunger strikers picketed the presidential residence to call for a constitution, or at the very least for a law that would change the rules.

But as this grassroots movement reached its peak, Yitzhak Shamir's Likud Party finally managed to put together a coalition with enough Knesset members to form a government. In the Machiavellian world of Israeli politics, it was too late – those in power had no interest whatsoever in changing the rules by which they had gained it.

THE PRESIDENCY

The presidency is the highest office in Israel. The nation's first president, Chaim Weizmann, was one of the most respected men in the history of Zionism. When he died in 1952, who but Albert Einstein was asked to succeed him. Einstein declined the offer, saying that he had "no aptitude at all for human relations," modestly adding that he only had "some understanding in the world of matter and nature."

David Ben-Gurion called Israel's presidency "the living symbol of the nation," but perhaps its most important role is not as a national symbol but as the representative of the national consensus and conscience. This was best exemplified in 1982 during the Lebanon War, when President Yitzhak Navon responded to the Israeli shock over the Sabra and Shatila massacres in Beirut by appointing a presidential commission to investigate the matter, an investigation which resulted in the resignation of Defense Minister Ariel Sharon.

But aside from such relatively rare interventions into Israeli political life, the role of the president is primarily ceremonial. Elected by the Knesset to a five-year term, the presidency is considered to be above politics, by and large out of the day-to-day tumult of national affairs.

There are some exceptions. The president has a more active role in the formation of a government during a coalition crisis, and he or

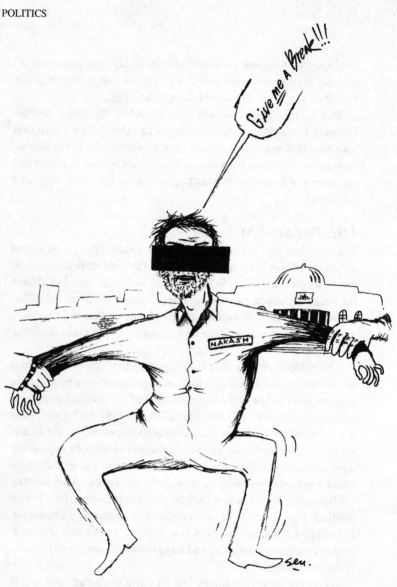

she has the power to grant pardons. But perhaps the president's most important contribution is the appointment of judges to the country's most remarkable institution, the Supreme Court.

THE SUPREME COURT

Israel's Supreme Court is the safeguard, if not the last bastion, of Israeli democracy. On many occasions, the court has acted at literally the last minute to correct a government injustice, limit political authority, or simply right a wrong.

A good example was the 1986 William Nakash court case. Nakash, who was French, managed to escape to Israel before his arrest for murder by French police. When the French government requested his extradition, he was arrested by Israeli security. However, before being sent back to France, his lawyers succeeded in convincing the Israeli justice minister that since Nakash was a Jew who had killed an Arab, his life would be in danger in a French prison. This "ideological" aspect of the case, like so many other issues in Israeli life, transformed what started out as a purely legal matter into a heated political conflict.

The far right adopted Nakash as some kind of hero, and the far left charged that in Israel "murder is somehow not murder" when it involves a Jew killing an Arab. In the midst of considerable publicity and headlines, the justice minister ruled for Nakash to be set free.

At the very hour when reporters (myself among them) were waiting outside the prison gates for his release, the Supreme Court acted. Nakash remained in prison, and the court heard his case. The result: the justice minister was overruled, and Nakash was extradited to France.

Supreme Activism

But this one example of the immediacy of the Supreme Court ignores its most remarkable attribute – its activism. There are very few areas of Israeli life, whether political, economic, or even mili-

65

tary, where the Supreme Court has not intervened. From Knesset elections to the conduct of the Israeli Army, the long arm of the Supreme Court has exerted its powerful influence.

During the Palestinian uprising, for example, when an infantry colonel was convicted by a military court of ordering the savage beatings of Palestinian youths, but was not sent to prison or even reduced in rank, the Court intervened. At the time of writing, the colonel is now a private, and he still faces a possible jail sentence. And when Meir Kahane, who formed a violently racist anti-Arab party, won a seat in the Knesset, the Supreme Court led the way in banning him from both the legislature and the election process, and used its influence to push the Knesset into eventually outlawing all racist parties.

The primary reason for the Supreme Court's overriding authority is derived not only from the great respect, if not reverence, with which it is held by the public, but from the very institutional problems which are the plague of the political system. Indeed, if the great weakness of Israeli politics is the lack of a constitution, then this is precisely what gives the court its immense power. Filling in the many gaps, the Supreme Court not only interprets the law but, through its many landmark decisions, has formulated Israel's ongoing, evolving "unwritten constitution." Not just deciding the law and striking new ground, Israel's Supreme Court acts as the rock in the fluid instability of Israeli politics.

THE THREAT OF FASCISM

Israel is a nation under tremendous pressure. The constant danger of war from Arab states, along with periodic terrorist attacks by hostile Arabs from the Territories, all come together to form an explosive mix which at times seems on the verge of blowing up.

Periods of instability bring tension, and in the pressure cooker atmosphere of the Middle East, emotions run higher than any place in the world. It's important to note that these threats are not imagi-

The last bastion of law – the Israeli Supreme Court.

nary but all too real. One only had to look at the United States in the McCarthy years of the 1950s to see how an imaginary threat – in the form of some omniscient internal Communist menace – nearly succeeded in undermining American democracy, and to understand how these threats pose such a great danger to Israeli democracy.

The lack of simple black and white solutions to the Arab-Israeli problem (and it's no coincidence that the Middle East is the longest lasting conflict in the post-World War II era) creates the dangerous phenomenon of politicians who *do* claim to have the simple answers – the strong men, the demagogues, and the preachers of hate; in short, all those who threaten Israeli democracy. And their principal weapon is always the same – racism.

Political Racism

Racism is the scourge of Israeli political life. After every terrorist attack – whether it be the Palestinian from the Territories who wreaks bloody havoc with a knife, or the Islamic fundamentalist from Lebanon, Jordan or Egypt who succeeds in getting through the border defenses and, with a cry of "Allah is Great," kills as many Israelis as he can – the tension and emotions which follow such events create what has become an inevitable, familiar scene: a crowd gathers, whether at the scene of the terrorist attack or at the funeral of the victims, and the hate-filled cry of "Death to the Arabs" is heard. Especially prevalent among the uneducated and the easily-influenced youth, the poison of racism often fills the air when periods of shock and unrest grip the country. With their many bitter memories of Arab anti-Semitism, the multitudes of Jews who emigrated to Israel from countries like Morocco and Tunisia are especially susceptible to the racist infection.

One of my best friends, born and raised in the small Jewish community of Tunis, came to know anti-Semitism not as country club exclusivity or whispered insults, but as being held down by six Arabs and spit upon. He, too, in the inevitable moments of shock and anger following a terrorist attack, will be heard forgetting his usual humanitarian political stance and say, "We have to take care of these Arabs!"

An Uphill Battle

Israel has tried to fight the epidemic of racism, but it's an uphill battle. One of the major victories was the banning of Meir Kahane's blatantly racist Kach party ("This Way" in Hebrew), but unfortunately it was soon replaced by a political movement called Moledet or "Homeland." The motto and indeed the entire philosophy of this party, which not only has two seats in the Knesset but whose leader is a minister-without-portfolio in the government, is "transfer." Here finally is the easy answer to all of Israel's problems. Simply take all the Arabs (the details are deliberately left unclear and vague) and "transfer" them to one of the Arab states (it does not seem to matter which one).

At the time of writing, Moledet has managed to get around the Knesset's anti-racism law, but the damage has already been done. That the Jewish state, which has some 300,000 survivors of the Holocaust among its citizenry, could come up with a political movement like Moledet is the cause of great pain to the vast majority of Israel's citizens.

The Extreme Right

The extreme right has also recently turned in a new direction: toward an alliance with ultraorthodox parties. It's well known in Israel that many of its ultraorthodox citizens (those who accept Israeli citizenship, that is) are not great lovers of secular democracy.

Believing that nationality and religion are one and the same, many of the ultraorthodox would prefer a theocracy, run according to the Jewish laws and customs of the Torah.

This familiar and not very daunting threat has existed since the creation of the state. What is new is that a significant number of secular voters have joined them.

With a mystical, almost tribal rabbinic leadership which claims to possess holy knowledge in political affairs, some ultraorthodox parties have managed to attract secular voters with their simplistic and often anti-Arab political stands.

The "spiritual leader" of one of these parties always appears in public wearing medieval robes (inexplicably accompanied by sunglasses), and in one of his more comic moments, excoriated the prime minister's wife as "evil" because of her preference for shrimps while dining abroad.

These fringe elements have joined forces with a growing number of religious Israelis who live on Jewish settlements in the Territories. For many of these settlers, religion and secular politics are bound together in an inseparable ideological mix.

Living on what they consider to be God-given land which is theirs by divine right, they have often come together with various right-wing and ultraorthodox parties in advocating the immediate expulsion of the Arabs, or other extreme measures to fight the Palestinian presence in the Territories. However, their principal demand is that Israel immediately annex Judea, Samaria, and Gaza, bringing them under Israeli law and into the Jewish state.

Without a doubt, the Territories pose the gravest danger to Israeli democracy. Even without the threat of annexation – which would bring 1.5 million angry Arabs into Israel – 25 years of military rule in the Territories have already left its shadow on the Israeli body politic.

The hundreds of thousands of Israelis who have done army service in the Territories have not only seen the workings of military rule with their own eyes, but have themselves played an active role in such an undemocratic system. Since 1967, the role of conqueror has become an inseparable part of the Israeli national personality, and this has not had the healthiest effect on the country's young democracy.

THE HOPE

But with all the fears, the threats and the worries, there always remains the hope. It's no coincidence that HaTikva ("The Hope") is the name of Israel's national anthem. It cannot be ignored that with all the massive pressures faced by Israeli democracy in the more than 40 years of its existence, it has not only managed to survive but has thrived, expanded, and grown.

For the vast majority of Israel's citizens, the many dangers have made them value and cherish their precious democracy all the more. Whether it be a free press that is one of the most aggressive, independent and combative in the world, or a level of political awareness and participation which is among the highest on the planet, Israeli democracy, like its people, intends to stay around for a long, long time to come.

Thomas Jefferson believed that the best medicine for any democracy is a revolution every five years. So it could well be that the very instability of Israeli politics is what will ensure its survival.

Chapter Four

A NEW CULTURE

"Delight in your youth, young man, make the most of your early days; let your heart and your eyes show you the way; but remember that for all these things God will call you to account."

—Ecclesiastes 11:9

ISRAELI CULTURE

One of the most exciting aspects of life in Israel is discovering Israeli culture. Here is an incredible and unique mix of the old and the new: a living language which is both one of the most ancient and one of the most modern on Earth; a world of literature, theater, art, dance and music which is still in its formative years; and surrounding it all a boundless enthusiasm which must have characterized all blossoming cultures in their first, most creative years.

Perhaps the most important Hebrew word in the entire history of Zionism is *chalutz* or "pioneer." For in Israel, it's possible to describe as pioneers not only Russian-born immigrants like David Greene – who in 1906 came to Turkish Palestine, changed his name to the Biblical "Ben-Gurion" and immediately set out to "build the land" – but also Israeli writers, artists, linguists, historians, philosophers, film directors, musicians, dancers and poets who in 1992 are still pioneering, breaking new ground, setting precedents and showing the way for generations to come.

Even a cultural field as seemingly minor as translation generates considerable excitement in Israel. Only in 1985, for example, was James Joyce's *Ulysses* published for the first time in Hebrew (just the first half; the second half was due in 1992). Its publication was greeted in the press by numerous excited and scholarly reviews, as if it was 1922 all over again when the book first came out. Except this time, of course, nobody was scandalized by the sex scenes!

THE HEBREW LANGUAGE

"Can you imagine buying a train ticket in Hebrew?"

This is the famous remark attributed, rightly or wrongly, to Theodore Herzl. For him, Hebrew was a 2,000-year-old sacred tongue suited only, like Latin in the Catholic Mass, to religious ceremonies.

His dream was of a Jewish state where the language and culture would be German (quite an irony, because Herzl would not live

73

The modernization of the Hebrew language; Moses would have been astonished to see Sprite advertised in the ancient language!

long enough to see German become instead the mother tongue of the Holocaust). If he was shocked by the thought of conducting business in Hebrew, imagine what he would have thought of today's myriad of Israeli advertisements for products as sublime as anti-acid and anti-gas pills, not to mention the Tel Aviv beach known in Hebrew as Tel Baruch ("Hill of the Blessed" is the ironic translation), which is the center of Israeli prostitution!

Eliezer Ben-Yehuda

It all began with a half-crazy, half-genius ideologue by the name of Eliezer Ben-Yehuda. Along with a handful of others, he was part of the famous initial wave of Zionist immigration to Israel which has since become known as the First Aliyah (1882–1903).

Immigrating in order to build a state, these were the very first Jews whose motives in coming to Israel were not religious but political. Yet Ben-Yehuda went one step further. Echoing the cardinal Zionist principle that the survival of the Jewish people depended on the creation of a national, political homeland, he asserted that this alone was not enough. Jews must somehow recapture their youth through a cultural as well as political rebirth. This could only be done, he declared, by rejuvenating the ancient Biblical language – Hebrew.

Ben-Yehuda, a true voice in the wilderness, was known to have walked through the streets of Jerusalem around the turn of the century and conducted his daily business in Hebrew, thus becoming the first human being to do so in more than a thousand years.

One can imagine the reaction he must have provoked from storekeepers, bankers, Turks, Arabs, not to mention his fellow Jews, who had never before heard Hebrew spoken in a non-religious context. According to historians, most people simply thought he was insane. But crazy or not, his revolutionary ideas caught on fast.

By 1911, there were already street demonstrations in Jerusalem calling for Hebrew to be made the official language taught in schools. And remarkably, Ben-Yehuda's children were the very first since Biblical times whose mother tongue was Hebrew. They were brought up from the cradle to speak the language, in an experiment which educators, sociologists and psychologists still marvel at to this day.

Through his teachings and writings, Ben-Yehuda's genius was that he succeeded in transforming Hebrew from a complex, labyrinthine and dying tongue into a simple, logical and modern language. Whether it be his reorganization of Hebrew grammatical structures, his creativity in inventing new words and phrases, or his brilliance in adapting ancient Biblical words to the daily workings of modern life, Ben-Yehuda laid the foundations for all of Israeli culture to come.

But what made him such a successful visionary was that he never forgot the reason for his work. His guiding principles were always simplicity and practicality, this for one very simple and practical reason: it would allow the hundreds of thousands of future immigrants in his vision to master their new language easily and quickly, with a minimum of pain and effort.

Indeed the spirit of Ben-Yehuda is alive and well today in Israeli classrooms, where more than ever before hundreds of thousands of Russians, Ethiopians, and other immigrants are studying Hebrew. The language school or *ulpan* ("studio" in Hebrew) is to the Israeli immigrants what Ellis Island was to the great waves of immigrants to the United States – that first shared experience on the long road to becoming a full-fledged citizen.

Language Schools

Israel has the largest number of language schools per capita of any country in the world; in every city and small town, on outlying border settlements and on the kibbutz. Even in the army, there are *ulpans*. And this is only the beginning, because with the massive wave of Russian immigrants now flooding the country, more and more language schools are being set up, and the call has gone out for more and more Hebrew teachers.

There are *ulpans* that are held in the morning, in the afternoon and in the evening. And who knows, what with the massive pressures of teaching hundreds of thousands of new immigrants, soon it will even be possible to attend an *ulpan* in the middle of the night.

Learning Hebrew

Learning Hebrew can in itself be great fun because it is, at one and the same time, a very simple yet strange language. For those accustomed to the Greco-Roman alphabet, it is a fascinating experience to begin to cope for the first time with a whole new form of writing, and to learn the meaning of those strange Hebrew letters which beforehand resembled some kind of cat scratchings. And above all, it really takes getting used to reading not from left to right, but from right to left. Like the Americans visiting England for the first time who rent a car and keep sliding into the driver's seat from the passenger side, it takes a while to get used to opening Hebrew books, newspapers and magazines from what you would normally think of as the back cover.

The ongoing development of the Hebrew language has been a fascinating story. A classic case in point is the word "telephone," which needless to say did not exist in Biblical times. Israel's prestigious Hebrew Language Academy, which meets every year to decide on additions and changes in the language, invented a word for the instrument, which roughly translates as "distance talker." But this Hebrew word with its purely Biblical roots, which the most esteemed linguists in the country worked so hard to come up with, has simply never caught on with the Israelis, and thus has never been used.

People instead just use the English word "telephone," and it's the same story with television and radio, not to mention video. Indeed, every year the purists of the language find more and more reasons to be disturbed; for them, the increasing anglicization of Hebrew is a cultural plague.

English is but one of the many foreign influences on the Hebrew language. New words have entered the Hebrew lexicon from the Yiddish, French, Russian vocabulary – in fact, from every country where immigrants have come. But one of the strongest influences has without a doubt been Arabic. Many Israelis say "Hi" in Arabic ("Halan"); and the Hebrew word for fun is not in Hebrew, but the Arabic "Kef."

However, Arabic's greatest contribution has somewhat ironically been in the area of cursing and swearing, a truly bountiful linguistic realm. Hebrew was found to be a bit weak in that department, so Arabic has generously stepped in to take up the slack. I won't bother translating some of the most popular ones, but suffice to say if you have the great misfortune of conducting a heated argument with an Israeli, some of the verbal barrage could well contain numerous uncomplimentary references to your, uh, mother's modesty.

Hebrew Names

Yet Hebrew is more than just the national language, it lies at the very heart of the Zionist ideal. The best illustration of this is found in Israeli names. For the nearly 20 years that Ben-Gurion was prime minister, he made it mandatory that anyone who worked in the government or in the public sector had to "Hebraize" their last name. That rule fortunately has been abandoned, so when working for Israel Radio, I was able to broadcast in the name my parents gave me, which I dearly wished to keep.

But nevertheless, there is a great symbolic significance to the act of changing names, just as there is real poetic beauty in many of them. For example, one of Israel's most famous war heroes is aptly named Meir "Har-Zion" (the Mountain of Zion); the name of the army chief of staff is Ehud "Barak" (Lightning); and the very appropriate name of one of Israel's most respected former presidents is Yitzhak "Navon" (Wise). For me, one of the Hebrew names which I will never forget is that of a fellow soldier from the Lebanon War to whom I owe my life. His name was "Israel Son of Lion."

ISRAELI LITERATURE

Israelis are among the most avid readers in the world. As you would expect from "the People of the Book," the percentage of people who buy books in Israel – whether best sellers, translations, or poetry – is much higher than that of the United States, England or France. In fact, UNESCO ranked Israel No. 2 in the world in book readership. (Iceland is No. 1.) This is an impressive statistic because publishing books in Hebrew for such a small population is not very profitable.

Israeli literature not only reflects the newness of the country, but the problems, the conflicts, and the soul-searching which are at the heart of the Israeli personality.

Freshness and relevancy are two words which come closest to describing what makes Israel's literature so unique – from the classic fiction of S.Y. Agnon, whose search for a new and elegant Hebrew style won him the 1966 Nobel Prize for Literature, to the Israeli authors of today like A.B. Yehoshua, Amos Oz and David Grossman, whose head-on confrontations with the Arab-Israeli conflict have won them a respected place in politics.

One of the most popular and controversial best sellers in the history of Israeli fiction is Yehoshua's *The Lover*. Focusing on the search for a missing soldier during the tragic aftermath of the 1973 Yom Kippur War, Yehoshua weaves a brilliant tale around the lives of an Israeli man, a woman, and a young girl who became involved with a young Arab. The Arab-Israeli conflict, in all its human dimensions, is presented in unforgettable fashion, with a simplicity of language and directness of style which is striking in its power.

The best-selling Israeli novel of all time is Oz's *My Michael*. In a style reminiscent of Agnon, Oz paints a wonderfully touching and

79

One of Israel's many used bookstores.

innocent picture of a young woman's life in Jerusalem in the decade after independence.

The climactic scene where she is reunited with her husband returning from the 1956 Sinai War is one of the most moving and unforgettable in all literature.

War, you will no doubt have noticed, is a subject never far from Israeli writing, whether it be fiction or poetry. Such is life in Israel, such is its culture.

FOREIGN LITERATURE

Israelis are also voracious readers of foreign literature. Not only are the major North American and European works translated into Hebrew, but many works from the more obscure and unknown writers of Africa, Asia, South America, and Eastern Europe are as well.

The changing demands of the Israeli market for different translations reflect worldwide cultural trends. During the 1950s, for example, the rage was for Russian classics by Tolstoy and Dostoievsky. In the 60s and 70s, the marked Americanization of the world saw a growing demand for classics from the United States. (Israelis, for some reason, were especially enthralled with William Faulkner.)

But particularly interesting are the translations which invariably pop up from time to time, seemingly without any logical reason. Whether it be Herman Melville's *Moby Dick*, which was only published in Hebrew in 1979, or the publication a year earlier of Norman Mailer's *The Naked and the Dead*, or even the recent new translation of T.S. Eliot's landmark poem *The Wasteland* (especially relevant to the multitude of Israeli war veterans), the examples are endless.

It's great fun browsing through the weekly literature supplements in the major newspapers to see which classic is going to be published soon in Hebrew, and then to read the reviews afterward.

It's almost as if the entire rich history of world literature is being relived all over again.

ISRAELI THEATER

To describe Israelis as great theatergoers is an understatement. Tel Aviv alone has three major theater companies, and besides the numerous theatrical productions in Jerusalem, Haifa and Beersheba, there are also community playhouses all over the country, even on the kibbutz.

Israel's National Theater, HaBima ("The Stage"), which began producing shows as early as 1922, presents three plays every day, six days a week, all year round. According to their statistics, 91 percent of their performances have been sold out.

Israeli theater is the true cutting edge of the national culture: original, powerful, and above all, political. Nothing is sacred to the Israeli playwright. From the Arab-Israeli conflict to the religious-secular dispute, every aspect of life in the country is fair game, even an issue as sensitive as the Holocaust. One of the most controversial plays in Israeli history was the Haifa Theater's 1984 production of Yehoshua Sobol's play *Ghetto*, a gripping drama of struggle, humiliation and courage in the World War II ghetto of Vilna.

Like Israeli literature, translation also plays a big part in the nation's theater. Whether it be a new Hebrew version of Chekov's classic play *The Cherry Orchard* (which recently made a tour of the country's kibbutzim), or the Haifa Theater's production in both Hebrew and Arabic of Samuel Beckett's *Waiting for Godot*, or even the National Theater's colossal staging of the Broadway musical hit *Cabaret* (this time, somewhat ironically, in Hebrew), translators, writers, directors, and actors have succeeded in making these international works somehow Israeli.

A good case in point is Arthur Miller's *All My Sons*, which in 1977 broke the record for the longest-running play in Israeli history. In his recently published autobiography, Miller relates how he once

The Israeli production of Arthur Miller's "All My Sons." (Picture courtesy of the Camari Theater)

attended what he describes as a tremendously powerful performance of the Hebrew production, and noticed how the audience was absorbed in the play with almost religious intensity. When he asked his host, then Prime Minister Yitzhak Rabin, about this, Rabin replied that the subject of the play – a businessman who knowingly ships out faulty aircraft parts during World War II – was similar to a problem in Israel. People at home were making money while soldiers were out on the front lines fighting. "So it might as well be an Israeli play," Rabin said.

Incidentally, the 1990 Hebrew production of yet another Arthur Miller play, *A View from the Bridge*, is at the time of writing still breaking records in Israel's theaters.

ISRAELI MUSIC

Nothing expresses Israel's unique personality more than its music, and one of the most pleasant surprises for any visitor to the country is that he or she could well fall in love with it.

From classical to folk to rock, one common enchanting element unites it all: that tinge of sadness which appears in virtually every work. This holds true for everything from the classical masterpieces of composer Paul Ben-Chaim – whose salute to the nation called *Fanfare to Israel* is at one and the same time glorious and haunting – to the folk songs of Yehudit Ravitz, whose beautiful voice strikingly resembles that of Joan Baez, but with an extra dose of bittersweet sadness.

Political Music

Music in Israel is also very political. From Yonotan Geffen's classic pop song *All Will Be Well*, which contains the controversial verse "If only we'll get out of the Territories," to Meir Banai's more recent hit *Rain*, in which he sadly calls for rain to come and "wash away the bad and make everything clean again," the political message is never far from the minds of Israeli songwriters.

Israeli rock star Yehuda Poliker in concert.

In the more than 60 years of Israeli music, with the multitude of songs about war, uncertainty and crisis, a recurring theme has always been that faint note of optimism, that sad plea to hold on until things get better.

A familiar refrain in one of the most famous Israeli songs is "Onward, we must keep going onward," which in itself is a very strong political message. It's no coincidence that this Rivka Zohar classic was one of the most played songs during the Gulf War, when the entire nation was glued to the radio.

Yet Israeli music is marked by more than just political relevancy. Cultural, ethnic and historical traditions are also very strong among musicians.

Two such people are Chaim Moshe, who went back to his North African roots to enrich the Israeli musical tradition with Arabic influences, and mainstream vocalist Hava Alberstein, who will occasionally depart from her usual Hebrew love songs to record an album or two in Yiddish.

But a true picture of the music scene in Israel would not be complete without mentioning the international influences. Jazz, fusion, punk, rock and even rap music are alive and well in Israel.

And not to be forgotten, yes, the country does have a rock singer who achieved legendhood, like Jimi Hendrix, Janis Joplin and Jim Morrison, by killing himself through drug addiction. His name, for those who are by chance interested, was Zohar Argov.

But it is much more appropriate to end this chapter on Israel's culture with a somewhat more praiseworthy example of music than the late Zohar Argov. Yehuda Poliker, one of the country's top rock stars, recently came out with a very powerful album, the theme of which is the Holocaust. (Not what you would think of as a subject very close to the hearts of Israeli youth, who are Poliker's main audience.)

However, Israeli music, like the whole of Israeli culture, is full of surprises, and in a series of moving rock songs, Poliker musically describes what it was like to grow up in a home in which both parents were Holocaust survivors. The name of the album, poetic in itself, is *Ashes and Dust*.

TIPS ON CULTURE

- A must for any visitor is to attend one of the many concerts held at Jerusalem's famous Sultan's Pool. This fantastic outdoor arena, sunken into a beautiful valley next to the walls of the Old City, is one of the most fabulous concert sites in the world. At night, with the Old City walls lit up in the background, the concert you attend – whether it be classical, jazz, pop or rock – will be an experience you won't forget.
- There are multitudes of free classical music concerts. Two of the most popular ones are at the Jerusalem YMCA, which is given every Thursday afternoon all year round (and are also simultaneously broadcast on Israel's classical music station), and in Haifa's Mount Carmel Park, which is held twice a week all summer long.
- In the English language newspaper, *The Jerusalem Post*, in all the other Israeli papers, in ticket agency offices in every city, and through the tourist information centers, you will find the weekly list of international artists appearing in Israel (and there are many), as well as concerts, plays, movies, film festivals, dance performances, book fairs, art shows, museum exhibitions, rock, jazz and folk music clubs – you name it. And don't forget to ask about tourist and other ticket discounts, and about special yearly subscription rates.

— Chapter Five —

THE ARMY IN ISRAEL

"The qualitative level of an army is a direct function of the level of the people, their sense of national identity, and their cultural and technological sophistication."

—David Eliazar, IDF chief of staff during the 1973 war.

MEETING THE ISRAELI SOLDIER

One of the most striking aspects of life in Israel, at least to the uninitiated, is the army.

On your first day in the country, perhaps while riding the bus, you will probably have your initial encounter with the typical Israeli soldier: unshaven, about 40, wearily trodding up the aisle in a rumpled olive green uniform which is completely indistinguishable, except for the three small Hebrew letters stitched in yellow above the breast pocket.

Strapped over one shoulder is a dingy, worn-out, brown duffel bag which looks like it has been in use since 1967, and as he trods down the narrow aisle, the bag brushes and knocks some of your fellow passengers. They, as well as he, don't seem to care or take much notice.

But it's what is slung carelessly over the other shoulder that provides the real shock – a machine gun. Perhaps it's an M-16, recognizable courtesy of television programs (or less sublime pursuits), or maybe it's one of the less familiar Israeli-made weapons.

The boy in you is tempted to stare at it, but before you know it, this "soldier" plops himself down on the seat next to you, drops the duffel bag on the aisle (oblivious that it's blocking the exit), stows the machine gun under his seat with an annoyed gesture that expresses the respect one might give a broomstick, and within minutes falls fast asleep.

Who is the IDF Soldier?

It's unfortunate but predictable that your first memorable encounter with the Israeli Army has been with a middle-aged reservist, though it could just as well have been with a beautiful young girl with an Uzi submachine gun casually slung over her shoulder like a purse; or perhaps more favorably with a clean-shaven young man with paratrooper wings on his chest and officer's bars on his shoulders. It's not just these singularly martial scenes on the bus or street

An Israeli soldier on his way home.

which take some getting used to. The army affects life in Israel in many other unique ways, some of them quite unexpected.

For example, after finally getting hold of that crucial business contact, or tracking down that long lost friend or relative, or locating the office of that elusive key bureaucrat, you may find taped to the door this note: "Gone to the Reserves – Back in a month."

In fact, one of the first Hebrew words you are likely to learn will be *miluim* or reserves, which is used even by non-Hebrew speakers to describe this often troublesome Israeli "lifestyle" that simply cannot be ignored. But of course the army is much more than that. It is, in the words of David Ben-Gurion, "a true people's army."

There are many distorted views of the Israeli Army or, by its proper name, the Israel Defense Forces (IDF). Mention it and varied images from the past come into focus: the famous photograph of the first paratroopers at Jerusalem's Western Wall during the war in 1967; thankful freed hostages with their rescuers after the Entebbe operation in 1976; and more recently, during the Palestinian upris-
, ing, far less glamorous pictures of Israeli troops with clubs and tear gas guns charging a crowd of Arab youths.

The real IDF, like the truth, lies somewhere in between. But before entering those gray areas, some black and white fundamentals. The most important characteristic of the Israeli Army, which differentiates it from most of the other armies in the world today, is its compulsory draft system.

THE DRAFT

In most of the developed world, the concept of the draft has negative, even evil, connotations for some and bad memories for others. For nearly a generation, the draft has largely become unknown because it has been replaced by all-volunteer armies. However, due to the militaristic stigma, volunteer armies are viewed by some with contempt, or mocked by others for being made up exclusively of the lower classes.

But in Israel, to put it simply, this is different. The military is for the vast majority a source of pride, and the draft is an integral part of the Israeli everyday life.

The Young Guns

At the age of 18, almost all Israeli men and women must enter the armed forces; the men serving for three years and the women two. A year earlier, Israeli high school students have to undergo medical examinations to receive their "military profiles." This is simply an examination in which every conceivable medical problem and physical trait of the potential draftee is taken into account, from less than perfect eyesight to flat feet.

To be selected for elite infantry units like the paratroops, for example, one would require a minimum score of 82, while to get into the tank corps (more sitting, less marching), only a 72 is needed. But to be an air force pilot, a perfect score of 97 is necessary. Wait a minute. Isn't 100 – not 97 – the perfect score? Not in the Israeli Army. The IDF considers circumcision a physical defect!

In any event, on the first day of their induction, the nation's youth, with their medical profiles in hand, report to one specific (and infamous) military base outside Tel Aviv where they are separated into a myriad of army, air force, and navy units. Several years later – and often about a lifetime older – these men and women return to the very same base to be discharged. For most, it is the happiest day of their lives.

The Future Soldiers

It would take a multitude of sociologists and psychologists to explain the effect that the draft – this inevitable looming prospect – has on the nation's young people, their parents, and the entire society. For the young, whether hearing about past army experiences from their parents or living through a similar period with older brothers and sisters, the focus of future plans often becomes

93

what to do in the army, in which branch to serve, and for which unit to volunteer.

This is an interesting twist. Jewish children around the age of 10 usually know exactly what they want to be – either a doctor, lawyer or professor. (Somehow it's never been quite enough for Jews simply "to be.") But in Israel, this syndrome has manifested itself instead with talk of being a tank officer, a fighter pilot or a crack paratrooper. Nevertheless, for Israeli youth there still remains this same career pressure, because the IDF is in many ways a microcosm of the civilian job market. One can become an army teacher, an army electrician, or even an army journalist. Others may choose, for example, to learn technical work in the air force, which offers excellent training for future civilian jobs.

For talented students, the IDF has an academic reserves program where they can delay their military service for a few years, study at the IDF's expense, and later serve in the army in their chosen field. It's also important to note that most of the elite of Israel's civilian society – the executives, general managers, and politicians – were officers during their regular army service, a fact well known to the young Israeli determined not only to succeed in the army but later in civilian life as well.

Coping with this sort of pressure can be exasperating for the 17-year-old who, on the verge of being drafted, wants to make the most of what he or she sees as the short time left to enjoy teenage life. This is one of the reasons why Israel's traffic accident rate is so atrociously high; freewheeling 17-year-olds are big contributors.

The Maturity Factor

Once in the army, it's an understatement to say that these kids grow up fast. It's amazing to see the changes and maturity these young people achieve after three years of army service; they don't look 21. Actually, it's a bit sad to discern such maturity on these young faces. As an immigrant, I was 26 when I served in the paratroops, and I thought my 22-year-old lieutenant and 23-year-old captain were much older than I was. Eli Wiesel often said that for him, the worst part of the Holocaust was that it deprived him of his childhood. Perhaps it can be said that for young Israeli adults, the worst part of the IDF is that it steals the best years of their youth.

Immediately after their discharge, many young Israelis choose to celebrate by traveling abroad. This is the reason why so many of them can be seen trekking throughout the world, with the inevitable backpack and weary Israeli smile.

Upon returning, the maturity which has been acquired in the army expresses itself in many ways. Israeli universities are filled with highly motivated students, most of whom already possess concrete career plans. Unlike many students in the United States, few Israelis go to university in order to "find themselves." After the experience in the IDF, they are more interested in academic and professional matters than in identity crises.

For parents, the army service of their sons and daughters can be an ordeal (especially on Jewish mothers). However, most Israeli parents handle it well, substituting their worry with pride in their children.

I remember once asking a middle-aged doctor what his son was doing in the army. "Oh, he's in the same unit that I was in," he answered proudly. When I asked him which unit that was, he replied evasively that it was an "elite" unit, and apparently such a good one that its name had to remain a secret.

There are undoubtedly many such units in the IDF, but if they were as numerous as proud parents insist their children are members of, then the Israeli Army would turn out to be the biggest "elite" military establishment in the world. But, of course, to parents, any unit that their children are a part of is an elite unit.

DIRECT INVOLVEMENT

By far the biggest part of being a parent to a son or daughter serving in the IDF can best be summed up in two words: direct involvement. When Israeli sons are serving on the Israeli-Lebanese border, news bulletins on the radio about a firefight there the previous night have more than just passing significance. Israeli society is extremely sensitive to this.

When I was working as a news editor at Israel Radio, in the middle of one of my first broadcasts, I received a phone call from the IDF spokesman announcing that three soldiers had been killed that morning in a training accident. There are few stories more important in Israel. So with three minutes to go before the end of the bulletin, I quickly rapped out a short news item, sprinted to the broadcast studio and, with 30 seconds to go before the bell, succeeded in handing the typewritten paper to the announcer, who read it with the dramatic introduction: "And this just in from the newsroom ..."

Victory, success, and a first-on-the-air scoop! Quite pleased with myself, I returned to the newsroom only to face an explosion. I had never seen the managing editor so angry.

In Israel, every such announcement must have the following sentence tacked on at the end: "The families of the soldiers killed have been notified." In the rush, I had forgotten this and my boss, who at the time had a son serving as an officer in an artillery unit, raged at me about this. I had caused thousands of Israeli parents to worry that perhaps it was their son who had been killed.

There are not many countries where such rules of journalism are mandatory, and it's one of the major tasks of the IDF censor to make sure that such announcements are delayed until after notification. In Israel, even the staunchest defenders of journalistic freedom support the censor on this.

Direct involvement also manifests itself politically. For example, parents with sons or daughters serving in the Territories (not to mention the tens of thousands of army reservists who serve there every year) are hardly apathetic toward the various political proposals on this issue, and have more than mere passive interest on it.

In the United States, they say that voters vote their pocketbooks. In Israel, it would not be an exaggeration to say that voters vote their lives, or the lives of their children.

THE INNER WORKINGS OF THE IDF

Besides the more conventional aspects of the Israeli Army – which is made up of the air force, the country's elite striking arm; the infantry and tank corps, the cutting edge of the IDF; and lastly the small but vital navy – it is possible to divide it into three main branches: the regular army (the kids), the reserves (their fathers), and most importantly the professional army, which makes the whole mechanism tick. In terms of size, the reserves is by far the largest branch, and is therefore the most critical element in the nation's defense.

In the event of a war, the maximum number of soldiers Israel can put into action is one of the nation's most important secrets, but suffice to say it's a good portion of the male citizenry. The last time there was such a full-scale mobilization was in the 1973 Yom Kippur War. As a result, the national economy was so crippled by the protracted call-up that it took many years for it to recover.

The regular army is of course much smaller, but if the reserves can be called the main body of the IDF, then the regulars are its backbone.

According to IDF doctrine, in the event of a war, it's the task of these youngsters to hold the front lines for 48 hours or more until the reserves can be brought into action.

Once again, it's the Yom Kippur War which provided the test, beginning with Egyptian and Syrian armies launching a surprise attack. In this war, the IDF plan worked, but at a terrible price. In the first 48 hours, the kids of the regular army managed to hold the line and in doing so, saved the country. But the action cost thousands of lives.

The Professionals

The professional army, made up of the senior officers, represents if not the heart of the IDF then certainly its brains. The best soldiers in the regular army are asked at the conclusion of their service to continue on as officers and "sign on" for at least one more year. The most outstanding of these progress through the ranks, and the best of the best become generals.

A career as an army officer in Israel is regarded as a true "higher calling," a sacrifice for national service which is highly respected by the citizenry. Israeli officers, noted for always being at the head of their troops into battle, are proud of their famous motto: "After Me." In all the nation's wars, they have taken a highly disproportionate percentage of the casualties.

Most of the country's leadership entered politics after climbing up the IDF ranks; Yitzhak Rabin and Arik Sharon are but two examples. Yitzhak Shamir became a politician by way of a different but no less respected path: the intelligence services.

Army Politics

As far as politics is concerned, the professional army, like the entire IDF, is non-partisan, and officers are sworn to steer clear of political issues. The army chief of staff, the country's highest ranked soldier, is considered, like the president of Israel, to be above politics.

But in a country as politically explosive as Israel, the task of remaining neutral is often like walking a tightrope. In the Territories, for example, the IDF declares that its job is to maintain order, thus allowing the political leadership to reach a solution. But this often works only in principle. Israelis, who are as familiar with the IDF generals as they are with the country's politicians, enjoy guessing which political party and ideological position a general supports. However, while trying to remain free of politics, the IDF is by no means free of criticism. Many senior army officers have been virtually crucified (sometimes unjustifiably) by politicians and the

One of the more attractive IDF sergeants. David Ben-Gurion once said that "the (Israeli) army represents a symbol of duty, and as long as (Israeli) women are not equal in this duty, they have not attained equality."

press for not living up to the extremely high standards expected of them. Every combat incident is not only investigated by the IDF but by an often cruel press as well, which seems anxious only to establish whether or not a mistake has been made.

The most bitter example was just after the Yom Kippur War, when several leading generals and even the chief of staff were excoriated and publicly disgraced for allowing the country to be surprised by the attacks.

The Women of the IDF

How does the IDF compare with other armies? There are many interesting differences, but one of the most noteworthy ones is the expanded role of women in the Israeli Army.

During an IDF training exercise, the first helicopter I ever flew in was, to my great surprise, piloted by a female air force lieutenant. And during my experiences in the jump exercises of the paratroops, an unlucky female air force cadet was designated to be the first to jump out of the aircraft. This was because, in the words of our chauvinistic instructor, "Who would chicken out after seeing a girl go first?"

Besides staffing most of the bureaucratic jobs which are so vital to the running of any modern army, there are also female tank instructors, military policewomen, technicians, and rescue workers (who were especially appreciated and praised by the public for their efforts during the Gulf War).

However, Israeli society, apart from the more revolutionary kibbutz movement, is still basically male-dominated and draws the line at certain points. Although they are instructors, women cannot serve in active infantry or tank combat units, and female air force pilots can fly support but not attack missions. Apparently, Israeli parents find it hard enough sending their sons off to battle; they have not yet come to grips with sending their daughters as well. Such, at any rate, is the mentality.

IMMIGRANTS IN THE IDF

One of the most original characteristics of the IDF is the role of immigrant soldiers. The compulsory draft system in Israel affects everyone, not just those born in the country, and army service is the price immigrants must pay for their citizenship.

Depending upon age, marital status and the number of children one has, immigrants serve from as little as a few months to the full three years for men and two years for women. In the crucial task of immigrant absorption, the IDF plays a key role; and perhaps more than any other institution in Israel, it is the army which is responsible for turning foreigners into Israelis.

IDF teachers conduct scores of Hebrew language courses. And before basic training begins, the army holds a special two-week program for immigrants to familiarize them with military life. These special courses make quick integration possible and, upon completing them, immigrants go on to serve in every conceivable unit in the army.

Germans, Ethiopians and Englishmen.

One day during the first two weeks of my time in the army, I was standing in line with about 30 other immigrants when our sergeant ordered in Hebrew for us to run into the nearest tent in 30 seconds. A long pause was followed by about six different languages asking the same panic-stricken question: "What does the Hebrew word 'tent' mean?" Having gotten the translation, we all stampeded like cattle into the newly learned word.

Our first lieutenant was, to say the least, the focus of unabashed awe by everyone. I myself could not quite fathom whether this tall, blond, Germanic-looking officer was really Jewish, until he tacked onto one of his verbal warnings about activities forbidden in the army the famous Yiddish term "Oy-Va-Voy." (If you get caught.)

A year later, I would serve with this same lieutenant under far different circumstances in Lebanon, and he told me that our first

A group of Ethiopian immigrants getting a taste of the army in a pre-induction course.

meeting had been his very first assignment after officer's school. The confidence he radiated!

He told me his funniest moment in the army came when one of the immigrants from England marched up to him, flashed an English, palms-out salute, clicked his heels in a style that would not have disgraced a Buckingham Palace guard, and in the thickest Manchester accent he had ever heard, blasted out in Hebrew a barely comprehensible "Yes, sir!"

The end of these first two weeks was no less memorable. Gathered around a blazing campfire the last night, an old man who was said to have lost two of his sons in Israel's wars, one in 1967 and the other in 1973, paid us a visit. He roared out to us in Hebrew: "Good that you've come!" After that night, most of us were mentally ready to join the Israelis arriving the next day to begin the grueling six months of basic training. Of course, the Israelis had no need for such encouragement, having already received a lifetime of it.

IDF TRAINING

The Israeli Army's approach to training its soldiers is interesting, if not unique. One thing you won't find in the IDF are screaming drill sergeants whose goal is to break down recruits in order to build them up as soldiers.

Combat units are all made up of volunteers, so motivation is about the last problem the army has to deal with. There is actually very little discipline in the IDF, hardly any saluting (in all my years I can only recall saluting once), and soldiers usually call their officers by their first names. Built on a different basis altogether, the following story provides a good example.

Choosing a Few Good Men

A friend of mine in the army reserves had the task of choosing recruits volunteering for the paratroops – not an easy job, because at that time only three soldiers were picked out of a pool of 30. There was only a short time to make the choice, so the idea was to bring every recruit to the point of physical exhaustion as quickly as possible.

Carrying loaded stretchers up and down sand dunes did the trick in no time at all, for – lo and behold – one of the smaller, skinnier fellows tottered, let out a groan, and fainted.

"Well," I later said, "that's one guy you don't have to bother with."

"No, he was one of the three that we picked," my friend replied. "Strength we can build up, but willpower and commitment we can't. By fainting, he showed that he had given his all."

It occurred to me afterward that perhaps only in the Israeli Army could one be accepted by passing out!

The Sleep Deprivation Factor

The guiding principles of IDF training can best be described as readiness and sleep deprivation. Readiness is of course the paramount factor, and learning how to cope with the pressure of always preparing yourself and your equipment for action, sometimes at a moment's notice, plays a big part. As a result, training often takes the form of frenzied activity lasting many hours and sometimes even for days on end.

I have experienced infantry exercises so pressurized that I actually recalled planning when I would have the time to roll up my sleeves! It takes a long time to learn how to function, and even how to relax under such conditions, without running around coiled as tight as a spring 24 hours a day. Indeed, success in coping with pressure is one of the most valuable lessons Israelis take away from their army service.

Sleep deprivation is crucial because the army, despite having endured several wars since, is still built upon the experiences of the 1967 Six Day War. In that war, Israeli soldiers fought for days and nights with hardly any sleep, grabbing whatever rest they could when they were being trucked or flown between different fighting fronts.

So for the Israeli soldier, the goal is to be able to fight virtually non-stop and with very little sleep for as many as six days. (Perhaps the Biblical account of toiling for six days and resting on the seventh is too important a concept to be forgotten by a Jewish army.)

In any event, training takes on a familiar, grueling weekly pattern. Every seven days is a world unto itself, building in intensity from the first day on, and reaching a climax, usually with an all-night march or maneuver, on Thursday night and Friday morning.

For the Israeli soldier, adjusting to sleep deprivation takes time. Like many struggles in life, it's primarily a psychological battle. At first, it is mentally crippling to begin a new day of training thinking, "Oh God, how can I go on after only two hours of sleep?"

But one soon discovers the lesson learned by insomniacs the world over – it *is* possible to go on, the world does not come to an end if you don't sleep, and the focus shifts to just making it to the end of the week and that blessed day of rest.

Indeed, one of the best things about the IDF is that soldiers go home at an extraordinarily high rate, usually at least once every two weeks. This frequent contact with family or the kibbutz – in short, the sane civilian world – is a great psychological boost to the soldier. Consequently, the bus stations on Friday are always jammed with soldiers heading home, exhausted but looking forward to the prospect of the Sabbath break which they have yearned for all week long. Then on Sunday morning, with clean uniforms and recharged spirits, these same faces flood the buses again to return to their bases for yet another period of training.

THE PRIDE AND THE PRICE

Without a doubt the most distinctive mark of the IDF is its pride, and the pride of the people in it. Having grown up in the United

States during the 1960s when Vietnam War veterans were jeered at, it was quite a change for me to see the military treated with such reverence and appreciation in Israel.

In fact, this is one of the best things about being an IDF soldier – it's hard to forget how ordinary men, women, and children look at you.

I have had old ladies give me candy on the street, schoolchildren visit me in the hospital, bus drivers ask me to settle disputes. During World War II, Allied soldiers on home leave must have enjoyed the same kind of gratifying treatment.

However, in Israel, this gratitude is tinged with sadness. In the center of every town is a memorial for the fallen sons and daughters of the country's wars, and the number of bereaved parents is terrible in its total. The price for this pride has been very high indeed.

TIPS ON THE ARMY

- It's against the law to photograph military bases.
- Take care about photographing soldiers in the street, especially officers, who can be recognized by the various assorted bars and insignias on their shoulders.
- It's encouraged, even considered patriotic, to pick up soldiers hitchhiking, which is one of their major forms of transportation while on leave. Be careful, however, about asking them specific questions like where their base is, because they are continually warned against divulging such information.
- Talking about the army, in social circumstances or otherwise, is not only perfectly all right, but a national pastime.
- Try to attend one of the swearing-in ceremonies of new

IDF soldiers, which are usually held at the Western Wall in Jerusalem. You are sure to hear about it from friends or acquaintances with children in the army. It's perfectly all right to attend, and is quite an interesting and moving ceremony. As you can imagine with typical parents, everybody photographs like mad.

- Don't forget, public transportation between cities is jammed with soldiers on Fridays, Sundays and on the day before and after holidays. It's by no means not recommended to ride the buses – indeed it can be a fun experience, provided you are not one of the passengers required to stand in the aisle on a long ride. But keep in mind that it's not like traveling during normal days.

Chapter Six

KIBBUTZ

"… the Lord said to Abraham, 'Look around from where you are toward north, south, east and west: all the land you see I shall give to you and to your descendants forever. I shall make your descendants countless as the dust of the earth; only if the specks of dust on the ground could be counted could your descendants be counted. Now go through the length and breadth of the land, for I am giving it to you.' "

—Genesis 13: 14-17

COMMUNAL SETTLEMENT?

Finally, there's a Hebrew word which defies translation. Kibbutz is defined in most Hebrew/English dictionaries as "an ingathering," and the closest further entries come to catching its meaning is the phrase "communal settlement."

But communal settlement is definitely not right; the entire philosophy of the kibbutz is built around a tremendous amount of work, leaving precious little time for "communing." Kibbutz, in English, should simply be called, well, kibbutz. An institution as revolutionary as this surely deserves its very own word in the English language. Only about 3.8 percent of the population currently lives on the kibbutz. Why then does it deserve its very own chapter in *Culture Shock! Israel*?

Kibbutz is first of all a major source of Israel's elite. Famous leaders like Moshe Dayan were born on the kibbutz, in the country's very first one, called Degania or "Grain Flower." And the father of the country, David Ben-Gurion, helped build a kibbutz in the Negev Desert, one of the country's most impressive, called Sde Boker, or "Morning Field." A high percentage of leaders – whether politicians, executives, or artists – either live on the kibbutz, or were born and raised on one. Yet perhaps the most telling proof of the link between the kibbutz and the Israeli elite is that an extremely high percentage of senior army and air force officers are kibbutz members. In a country where distinguished military service is the number one requirement for admission into the elite, this says a lot.

The Importance of the Kibbutz

The importance of the kibbutz can clearly be seen in the sheer physical geography of the country. On your map of Israel, many of those dots with Hebrew names spread out across the land and filling up the empty spaces are not small towns and villages but kibbutzim. There are some 300 of them – not an insignificant number in a nation as small as Israel. Outside of the major cities, it is the kibbutzim which dominate the landscape, making an indelible mark on the personality of the country.

But above all, the kibbutz movement has played a leading role in the political, economic, and social history of the state. The most innovative form of Zionism, the kibbutz has won worldwide fame as Israel's most revolutionary phenomenon. In short, it is virtually impossible to understand Israel, its people and its mentality, without understanding the kibbutz and its development.

THE PIONEERS

It all began with a bunch of crazy Russians. Immigrating to Israel between 1904 and 1919 in what has become known since as The Second Aliyah, these men and women were ideologues, strongly influenced by the political and social turmoil of Russia in the throes of the 1905 and 1917 revolutions.

Radical socialists, utopian collectivists, call them what you will, these immigrants were determined to build in Israel not only a new political entity (like Herzl) and a new cultural center (like Ben-Yehuda), but a new social order as well; to create not only a modern state and culture, but a unique socialist society built upon the twin ideals of equality and work.

A revolutionary economic system which would be the opposite of the old model of European colonialism, they believed that everyone should participate in the labor of society, not by exploiting one another but by doing the work themselves. It's a bit mind-boggling to picture these Jews – most of them young men and women full of socialist dogmas and theories – against the stark reality of what Israel actually was in the first decades of this century: a wild, barren, rock-strewn land with scattered Arab villages, Turkish rulers, very little water, hardly any shade, and a lot of diseases.

These pioneers were not just parroting the socialism of Marx and Engels. Once their lofty principles met the harsh realities of life in Israel, something new and exciting emerged out of the mix. The

A.D. Gordon's famous hoe, with one of today's kibbutz members on the end of it.

best example of this was the most famous of all the socialist dreamers of the Second Aliyah, a man named A.D. Gordon.

Gordon's Dream

Resembling a typical Russian peasant with his long beard, A.D. Gordon is seen in photographs bent over the fields of Israel's first kibbutz, Degania, with a hoe in his hands. In fact, he could well go down in history as the only political theorist ever to build an entire economic and social philosophy around that very same hoe.

Like Ben-Yehuda, who believed that a modern, revived language was needed in order to "rejuvenate" the Jewish people, Gordon declared that only physical labor on the land of Israel could heal and purify Jews returning to their homeland. "Hebrew work," as he called it, was not only a means to an end, but an end in itself. Physical labor was the highest value in life, and the link between man and nature through "the conquering of work" would bind the settlers to their new land. This also had immediate political implications. Gordon argued that if the returning Jews failed to take up this philosophy, they would become typical colonialists, exploiting the cheap labor of the village Arabs to do their jobs.

Degania

Believing in this new creed, in 1910, a group numbering a mere 12 people gathered on the shores of the Sea of Galilee to create Degania, the mother of all kibbutzim. As in many remarkable endeavors, very little was actually planned in advance.

Although some of the earlier European and American experiments in communal settlement were known and perhaps did have some influence, most of the first developments at Degania and other pioneering kibbutzim were practical rather than philosophical.

For example, one of the most basic tenets of kibbutz life – that the workers are not employees but collective owners of the settlement – developed mainly because of lessons learned from the prepopulation of some 1,400 people, a variety of agricultural crops, four separate factories, an educational center, swimming pool, cultural center, museum, zoo, the works.

But with all its impressive development, what still remains is the simple image of A.D. Gordon and his hoe. And it's an image that has become legendary. The United States has its cowboys, England its Knights of the Round Table, and Japan its samurais. Israel has pioneers like Gordon who, with their overeducated heads full of socialist ideas, simply and joyfully worked the land doing the physical, manual labor of peasants. It's a legend that has become an integral part of the Israeli mentality.

One of the great ironies of Israeli history is that in 1909, a year before the establishment of Kibbutz Degania, the other great achievement of the Second Aliyah took place: the foundations were laid for the first Zionist city – "Hill of Spring," or Tel Aviv.

What is the irony in that? The irony is that in all the volumes of Zionist philosophy which constitutes Israel's ideological legacy, from books about how Jews once forbidden to own land would now work with their hands as farmers, to pamphlets about tilling the soil and making the desert bloom, little if anything at all was written about the role of the city in modern Israel.

Ironic too that these Russian-educated Zionist philosophers, so familiar with socialist thought, gave so little consideration to the question of industrialization. They were simply convinced, like Mao in China later, that the economy of their country would always remain agricultural. Perhaps they were right in thinking that the massive task of industrialization would certainly be beyond the future nation's means. Where would the money come from? If they could have known the answer, it would have saddened them greatly. The money for Israel's industrialization came from repentant West Germany, which in 1950 decided to establish diplomatic relations with Israel, and acknowledge the Holocaust by agreeing to pay nearly $1 billion in war reparations.

vious failures in conventional farming management, rather than as a result of any intentional ideological program. The children's house, one of the most revolutionary aspects of the kibbutz, came about not because of any social or educational consideration, but simply because, in those first difficult days, all the children were housed in the one strong, sturdy building which was built to withstand the rages of weather, malaria, and the threat of unfriendly Arabs. The philosophy behind these radical developments, which would turn a practical experiment into a way of life, would come after those stormy first days.

Degania began a wave of kibbutz settlement that spread across Israel and became the crowning achievement of those early years of the Second Aliyah. The work was extremely hard; clearing the land of rocks and boulders, building houses, devising new methods of irrigation, and planting crops was difficult enough physical labor. Yet on the central coastal plains and in northern Galilee, the Herculean task of draining the swamps was added, for the mosquitos which bred in them caused massive malaria epidemics which ravaged the new settlers. It is no wonder David Ben-Gurion wrote that some 90 percent of the immigrants of the Second Aliyah could not make it, and after a year or two of backbreaking labor, they left the country.

However, those pioneers who stayed planted the seeds of the kibbutzim of today, and indeed of much more than that. When those first pioneering settlements came together to form a united kibbutz organization, they were laying the foundations for Israel's first political parties.

The Legacy

Degania today is one of the most successful and beautiful kibbutzim in the country. In fact, it is now two separate settlements: the original one called Degania Alef (A), and the second one, which begun in 1920, called Degania Bet (B). Together, they have a

In one of the most controversial and bitterly fought battles in Israel's political history, David Ben-Gurion succeeded in convincing the Knesset to accept the money. Israel was industrialized, and one of the inevitable results was the gradual decline of the kibbutz and its ideology from its once dominant place in Israeli life.

THE KIBBUTZ WAY OF LIFE

No money, no bills, no rent, a total democracy with equal rights and sexual equality, the true utopian "city on the hill" – the mythology of kibbutz life has gained international fame. Does the legend really live up to the reality?

In many ways, the answer is yes. Money and all of its vexing

115

accompanying baggage really does not exist on the kibbutz, at least in the formal sense. Consequently, one of the greatest pleasures in kibbutz life is to take that cumbersome leather wallet from your purse or trouser pocket, thick with its credit cards, checkbook, cash (hopefully), identification, and other items of modern life, and put it away in the back of the closet where it belongs. If your definition of freedom is "freedom from the wallet," then the kibbutz is definitely for you.

Kibbutz Monetary Solutions

How can any society function without money? The kibbutz has come up with some interesting alternatives. Since all the property on the kibbutz are owned by members, everything from houses, main buildings and cars to the books in the library and the food in the kitchen belongs to everyone. So depending on your point of view, the kibbutz member is either the owner of a tremendous amount or of nothing at all.

The kibbutz decides democratically where the annual profits should go, whether into building a new children's house, for example, or purchasing airline tickets for travel. All the basic necessities of life – food, clothing, health and educational costs, travel needs, even "culture" (concerts, films, books, a television and stereo set for each member, all considered by the kibbutz to be basic necessities) – are free.

At the food or clothing store of the kibbutz, each member has a personal account, and he or she simply goes in, takes whatever is wanted or needed, and signs for it. No money, God forbid, changes hands. Even the act of signing is a relatively new kibbutz procedure, a deviation from those pure earlier days when someone like Gordon would of course never go over budget!

The kibbutznik (which is Hebrew slang for the kibbutz member) only handles real money when occasionally traveling to the big, bad city in order to make some exotic purchase. If, for example, the urge to go to Tel Aviv and buy something at one of the new shopping malls hits the kibbutznik (old A.D. is naturally shaking his head in stern disapproval), he or she can withdraw cash from the "personal budget," which is a fixed amount of money held in account for those needs somehow not covered by the all-inclusive kibbutz lifestyle. I discovered while living on the kibbutz that a good example of one such "need" was for Johnny Walker scotch; the kibbutz unfortunately remained unconvinced that it was a necessity.

Kibbutz Democracy

Kibbutz democracy, in principle and practice, is where the reality of kibbutz life comes closest to the legend. Every decision is voted on, from who is accepted as a member to whether films will be shown on Monday or Wednesday night.

Kibbutz democracy takes place six nights a week – six and not seven, because Friday nights are reserved for the big cultural event of the week, whether it be a theater performance, a concert, or a party – and only at night because nights are when the committee meetings take place.

After the normal day's work, every evening there is a committee meeting, whether it be the work, health, education, security, sports or culture committee, or even the "secretariat" committee, which oversees the entire apparatus. (It is no coincidence that many of the kibbutz terms sound Russian.) In these committees, voting takes place, but only as a preliminary step; the final decisions are taken at the weekly kibbutz meeting.

All roads in the kibbutz democracy lead to the kibbutz meeting. Once a week, hundreds of people on the older kibbutzim come together in a big meeting hall with microphones and a stage. On the smaller, newer (and naturally poorer) kibbutzim, a few dozen members gather in the dining hall after all the dishes are done and the tables wiped clean.

At the meeting, every issue is discussed, debated, sometimes fought over, and ultimately voted on. As to the procedures, the kibbutz movement has developed an intricate set of parliamentary rules worthy of the British House of Lords, including quorums, agendas, motions, voting rules, and even "points of order" (shades of Joseph McCarthy).

If a decision is, as it is known in the kibbutz jargon, a "decision of principle" (principle being the most sacred word in the kibbutz vocabulary), then a simple majority is not enough. It must be approved by a two-thirds vote. Except that a decision of principle on the kibbutz can be anything from employing salaried workers from outside the settlement (an anathema to the old-timers) to the earth-shaking question of whether or not dogs on the kibbutz be put on a leash. "After all," someone will say, "it's an issue of quality of life, which is a kibbutz principle."

So each week these Israeli farmers, many of whom must get up the next morning at around 4:30 a.m., are often at it until well past midnight, fighting it out and demanding their say (sometimes several says), and somehow managing to inexplicably link the issue of dog leashes with Herzl, Gordon, Stalinism, the French Revolution, and universal rights.

Kibbutz Kids

So much for kibbutz democracy, you say, but how could any sane self-respecting parent agree to put their precious child in a children's house at night? This is the usual reaction of those unfamiliar with kibbutz life, and it's not only a matter of culture shock, because many Israelis also ask the very same question. Yet the children's house concept is not quite as bad as it sounds.

Every day, when 4 p.m. rolls around, the kibbutz child goes straight home (their parent's home, that is) and the family is together until it is time for bed. Then the parents take their kids to the children's house, go through the entire nighttime ritual, from the bedtime story and last cup of chocolate milk to the goodnight kiss,

The Children's House on a kibbutz.

and then depart, leaving them in the competent hands of the children's house supervisor and night guard, who do not hesitate to call if anything is wrong.

The philosophy behind the idea is that each afternoon, when the children are reunited with their parents, those several hours together are transformed into "quality time." For the entire family, the reunion becomes "an event" rather than mere routine. The kids are on their best behavior, and the parents make a more conscious effort to concentrate on their child's real needs. Such, in any case, is the theory, and my experience on the kibbutz has been that it may well be true.

As far as the effects of growing up in the children's house are concerned, psychologists, sociologists, and educators extol the virtues of what is at the heart of the kibbutz ideology: the group rather than the individual concept. Research on this is still being done, and the final verdict is not yet in. However, very little guesswork is required to appreciate the benefits of the system for the kibbutz parents. Each and every night after the children are in bed, they are free to continue with their lives, released from the bonds which tie most parents down to their homes.

Kibbutz Women

Sexual equality is by no means completely achieved on the kibbutz, but it's fair to say that kibbutz women are far more liberated than their contemporaries in the rest of Israeli society.

One of the main reasons is without doubt the children's house concept. Except for the first few months following the birth of her child, when baby and mother are together at home 24 hours a day, the kibbutz mother soon finds herself free to return to her normal life. This could well include university or other professional training. Indeed one of the most impressive statistics on the kibbutz is the fixed percentage of members, male and female, who are sent to study each year. And it's important to note that this has been going on for as long as the kibbutz has existed, which is a lot longer than the 25 years or so since the large-scale liberation of modern women. As with the other revolutionary aspects of kibbutz life, the developments have largely come about due to practical rather than ideological considerations.

On my kibbutz, for example, the secretary (and I mean the president of the kibbutz, not the typist) was a woman, as were the chief economic planner and the head of the vineyard. This happened not as a result of any "decision in principle," but simply because they were the most qualified people available at the time.

On the other hand, just so that you are not left with the impression that my kibbutz is somehow ideally cut off from the still overwhelming global social trends, 99 percent of the work force in the children's house and the kitchen still remains female.

THE CHANGING KIBBUTZ

The modern kibbutz movement is going through a period of crisis. Economic difficulties, worries over a negative growth rate in population, and shifting social trends have all resulted in radical changes in the traditional kibbutz lifestyle. These changes have themselves caused serious problems, which go to the heart of the question of what the kibbutz is all about. And the crisis is serious enough that the one all-important question has even been raised: Can and will the kibbutz survive?

The Profit Factor

One of the major dilemmas of the kibbutz today is the simple but inescapable fact that even an institution as socialistic as this must still make a profit in order to survive. And here, one can't avoid the inevitable comparison to the landslide decline of socialism worldwide.

In Israel, the major problem has been the long-lasting unprofitability of the agricultural sector, which has left many kibbutzim deep in debt with serious financial troubles. As a result, after years of struggles, the kibbutz movement has begun to concentrate on a phenomenon unknown and indeed unthinkable during the early years – the kibbutz factory.

Nearly every kibbutz in the country has learned the bitter lesson that the hard cash needed to pay the bills will never be made on agriculture alone, leaving no alternative but to expand into the industrial sector.

On my kibbutz, for example, the economic future depends not on the apple orchards, the corn harvest, the chickens and the cattle, but on the factory which manufactures telecommunication cables.

But this solution has caused serious social conflict. Many kibbutz members object to working in a factory, which they consider to be a far cry from the ideological heart of what the kibbutz should be.

"Why did we come to the kibbutz?" they ask. "To push buttons inside a factory, or to work the land with our hands?"

Yet economic pressures have forced many kibbutzim to put more and more of their members into the factory, and to press for increased productivity by proposing incentives as averse to kibbutz ideology as increasing the personal accounts of those members who work overtime. Even the question of introducing salaries is being debated in many kibbutzim. Such proposals have often succeeded not only in pushing members into the factory, but right off the kibbutz itself.

Decline in Membership

But without doubt the greatest threat to the future of the kibbutz is the marked decline in membership. More and more of the young people born and raised on the kibbutz have decided not to return to the settlement after their army service, and have headed instead for the big cities. The average age of the kibbutz member has consequently risen higher and higher each year, and there is a growing concern that the next generation may well be the last. Ironic that in these times when Israel is being flooded by huge immigrant waves, the most serious problem for the kibbutz is attracting new members. But unfortunately for the kibbutzim, the vast majority of these immigrants are Russian Jews, who see a connection between the kibbutz philosophy and the Communist theories from which they have fled. Somehow believing that the kibbutz must be akin to one of Stalin's forced labor camps, they are about as attracted to kibbutz life as ultraorthodox rabbis are to pork.

The struggle to attract new membership has often eroded the traditionally cherished values of the kibbutz. One such example is the decision of many kibbutzim to "increase their appeal" by allowing members to work in their chosen professions outside of the kibbutz.

The strategy has worked, and many kibbutzim have succeeded in recruiting lawyers, businessmen and other professionals who leave the settlement every morning for work in a nearby city. However, many wonder whether a kibbutz where members live but don't work together truly remains a kibbutz. Even the sacrosanct children's house has been dropped by many, who see it as an obstacle to attracting potential members frightened off by the concept.

The Crisis of the Kibbutz

Thus the crisis of the kibbutz has become twofold: first of all, to survive, and second, to survive as a kibbutz. In an institution where ideology plays such a central role, the conflict between these two often contradictory goals may well prove to be insurmountable.

Whatever the fate of the kibbutz, one can't help but believe that, like similar gloomy predictions about the future of Israel, the doomsday theories will prove premature. The one and only kibbutznik will always remain: that rare animal in a blue work uniform (Mao's legions wore black, the kibbutznik wears blue), whose afternoon nap from two to four is more sacred than any religious shrine, and whose schedules and duties (work schedule, vacation schedule, use of car schedule, committee schedule, dishwashing duty, dining hall duty, children's house night supervisory duty, night guard duty, sabbath work duty, sabbath dishwashing duty, sabbath dining hall duty, sabbath children's house supervisor duty and other schedules) go on and on and on. The future of the unique phenomenon known as the kibbutz may well prove to be as long as the never-ending schedule/duty lists eternally posted on the kibbutz bulletin board.

TIPS ON THE KIBBUTZ

- Visiting a kibbutz is, of course, a must. Many of the more successful kibbutzim have expanded into tourism, offering first-rate hotels and bed and breakfast lodging. Most are quite nice – but these are recommended more for use during trips and tours around the country than for getting a real taste of kibbutz life.
- Many kibbutzim have volunteers, and if you have some time on your hands, it's quite easy to become one. Volunteering on the kibbutz is an experience not so much Israeli as it is European, because the vast majority of volunteers are young Europeans who flock to Israel during the fruit-harvesting season.
- Work can often be quite hard, as can be the itinerant young European lifestyle. However, if you want to give it a try, addresses and phone numbers of big kibbutz organizations in Tel Aviv can be obtained through any tourist center, or even in the English yellow pages. These organizations can make all the necessary arrangements for volunteering.
- There are three major kibbutz organizations in Israel, so

you can take your pick according to your political or religious inclination. The largest is the United Kibbutz Movement, which is aligned with the Labor Party. Next comes the Religious Kibbutz Movement which (you guessed it) is religious and usually right wing, with many kibbutzim in the Territories. Last but not least is the Kibbutz Artzi ("country" is the rough translation of the word), which is aligned with the secular left.

- But the best way of getting a look at the kibbutz is to hopefully receive an invitation to visit from a friend or business acquaintance. With hope, it will be a kibbutz without volunteers (my experience has been that kibbutzim with volunteers tend to be less friendly, accustomed as they are to putting up walls between themselves and strangers).

- Weekends are a good time to visit, but holidays are the best. The kibbutzim put their own special touch on the holidays, which makes the visit an unforgettable experience. Even better, try to get an invitation to stay a week, then you can work (hopefully not in the factory), attend a kibbutz meeting or two, and discover what it's like to become an infamous kibbutznik!

Chapter Seven

SECURITY

"He who ordains the order of the universe will bring peace to us and to all Israel."

—Arthur Hertzberg, *Judaism.*

AWARENESS

When reading the newspaper, listening to the radio or watching television, one can easily get the impression that Israel is one of the most dangerous places on earth.

In the United States there are 24,000 murders a year, but in Israel, when one lone Palestinian terrorist kills a civilian, there are banner headlines worldwide, and film crews rush to the scene to shoot some much demanded video footage, soon to be televised everywhere from Finland to Fiji. Of course, when the terrorist declares that his motive was neither money, sex, nor pure craziness but nationalism, patriotism or religious fundamentalism, the killing is no longer considered an ordinary crime, but an integral part of the Arab-Israeli conflict – worthy therefore of inflated journalistic coverage.

The Real Story

For those coming to live or work in Israel, it becomes extremely important to put the question of security into its proper perspective. It's a pure and simple statistical fact that you will be much safer in Israel than in the majority of the major cities on the planet; safer than Paris, safer than London, and certainly safer than New York.

Crime is extremely low here. There are no muggings and no street gangs; and when night falls, Israelis are not prisoners in their own homes, as it's possible to walk the streets at all hours with virtually no fear of assault whatsoever.

Another important part of putting things in perspective is the realization that most of those blaring news headlines about Israel – whether it be a firefight on the border or an incident in the Territories – do not touch the lives of the average Israeli. It's often hard to convince those unfamiliar with the country and its geography that, for example, the Jabaliya Refugee Camp in Gaza, the site of rioting and stone throwing, is not exactly what you would call Main Street, Israel.

Security personnel checking a customer's bag before she is allowed to enter the store.

But it's impossible to deny that security is a fact of life in Israel as it is in no other country in the world. From your first moments at Ben Gurion Airport, if you unwisely decide to stow your luggage in a corner somewhere unattended for a few minutes while making a quick dash to the washroom, upon returning you are likely to find a very surprising scene indeed: police evacuating the building, the bomb squad already called in and on the way, and the entire focus of all this urgent, dangerous activity centered on none other than your familiar, somewhat pathetic little suitcase.

Security awareness (and throughout this whole chapter the key word will be "awareness") is higher in Israel than anywhere else in the world. Whether it be opening your purse, briefcase or backpack for the careful inspection by a security guard at the entrance to every imaginable public facility from the grocery store to the theater, you will quickly discover that the question of security is as normal and natural a part of daily life as the weather and the time.

Yet for the newcomer, security can be a curious and even frightening experience – a big part of that initial culture shock of being in Israel. However, after a short time in the country, you will quickly find yourself, like the rest of the Israelis, not giving a second thought to all the extra precautions. And those few important security considerations that do have to be kept in mind will soon become second nature.

GETTING HERE

Your first encounter with Israeli security will no doubt be on your flight into the country. Although seasoned international travelers are all too familiar with the vexing routines of airport security, as far as flying to Israel is concerned, you will discover that, as the saying goes, "you ain't seen nothin' yet."

By Air
For obvious reasons, Israel has always led the way in airline secu-

rity, setting the standards which other countries have unfortunately found it necessary to imitate. The sad fact is that security must still be the first consideration of any traveler flying to Israel.

So even before getting here, you must already begin to think like an Israeli; which means the primary consideration in choosing your airline should not be the beauty of the flight attendants, the amount of free drinks or the quality of the food, but rather the far from appetizing question of security. And as far as security is concerned, the Israeli carrier, El Al (meaning "On High" in Hebrew), is simply the best and safest airline in the world.

Flying El Al

But there is a price to be paid for safety. No passenger on El Al will ever claim that the quality of the food and service reminds them of Singapore Airlines (although some of the Israeli flight attendants don't compare too badly with their Singaporean counterparts).

In any case, you will bear the principal burden of all the added security well before getting onto the plane and into your seat. El Al requests that all its passengers arrive at airports to check in at least two hours before the scheduled departure, and with the myriad of security procedures, there is very little problem in filling up the time. Unlike other airlines, the El Al ticket counter is not your first stop but rather your most yearned for objective; getting there can sometimes take more than an hour.

Most of the delay is caused by the preliminary luggage check, in which your bags are searched by security personnel in your presence, who will ask you a variety of questions at the same time. Indeed, for those unfamiliar with El Al, one of the most unexpected aspects of their security is the many questions, which sometimes are a lot less self-explanatory than the obvious "Did any stranger give you a package to put in your suitcase?"

So a good rule to keep in mind to prepare yourself for this procedure is to be ready for some interesting queries. And above all, be patient. Like an orange which has been squeezed for juice not once, not twice, but three times, when you finally succeed in boarding the plane and taking your seat, you could very well find yourself feeling a bit wrung out. But it's worth it; the feeling of safety and security El Al gives its passengers is without doubt one of the nicest parts of its service.

By Sea and Land

There are, of course, many other ways to get to Israel. Like the immigrants of old, you can cruise into the port of Haifa by ship, a romantic and not inefficient way to travel. It's also possible to take the overland route via Egypt or even Jordan. This is usually the choice of those economizing passengers intent on taking advantage of the cheaper air fares to Cairo or Amman, who then continue on into Israel by bus.

Will I recommend these from a security point of view? Well, it's difficult to say. Fatalists with a tendency to throw caution to the wind will no doubt skip this section, so I will address the more conservative traveler.

In the Middle East, there have been terrorist attacks on board ships (the 1985 hijacking of the luxury liner *Achilles Lauro* being the most infamous). Jordan is a country which remains in a state of war with Israel, and terrorist attempts to infiltrate the border have been on the increase in recent years.

As far as Egypt is concerned, despite the peace with Israel, a more fitting description of relations between the two countries would be a kind of long-lasting cold war. Those traveling to Israel via Cairo and then across the Sinai peninsula by bus should keep in mind that the rising tide of Islamic fundamentalism in Egypt has created a problem.

So what's the bottom line? Call me a cowardly jellyfish, but the bottom line is that from a security point of view, the safest way to travel to Israel is to fly here, preferably with El Al. Period.

THE ISRAELI VIEW OF TERRORISM

Israel has been dealing with terrorism long before it was even known as terrorism. In the pre-independence days before statehood, bombings and other indiscriminate acts of violence against civilians were much greater than they were later.

One of the worst of these attacks took place in March 1948, two months before independence. Arab terrorists succeeded in exploding a car bomb in the courtyard of the West Jerusalem building which housed the Zionist leadership. Thirteen people were killed, but fortunately for Israel, David Ben-Gurion was not one of them.

But terrorism, as it is known today, only really entered the modern lexicon in the late 1960s. Across the globe, with hijackings, bombings, grenades and machine guns, this "new wave" shook the world, capturing international headlines and confronting politicians with a new and frightening reality which became known simply as terrorism.

Continuing to gather momentum in the 1970s, terrorism reached its peak in Israel in 1972 with the bloody Lod Airport attack, in which Palestinian-trained Japanese terrorists killed 26 people (to this day, the worst terrorist strike in Israeli history); and once again in 1974 with the slaughter of 20 schoolchildren in the northern Galilee town of Ma'alot.

The Turning Point

In the war against terror, Israel has found itself in an unceasing battle against an enemy whose goal is neither military nor political victory, but instead to shock, stun and terrify. And of course it's a phenomenon which has spread like cancer far beyond Israel's borders – from the 1972 Munich Olympics massacre, to the 1976 hijacking of an Air France jet to a little known airport in Uganda called Entebbe. At Entebbe, however, something new and revolutionary took place – Israel mounted a daring commando operation and rescued the hostages.

Entebbe was a true turning point in Israel's long war against terrorism. The victory by the Israeli commandos, led by the late Yonotan Netanyahu (who was killed in the rescue and whose brother, Benyamin, is now one of the country's leading politicians), showed the world for the first time that impotence and frustration were not the only answers to terrorism.

In fact, since the Entebbe operation, through the 1980s and up until the present day, terrorism in Israel has declined markedly. This has not happened as a result of any decrease in attempts by terrorists, but simply because Israel has succeeded in learning the hard lessons of how to fight terrorism, and how to prevent it.

A Continuous Battle

It's a continuous battle, as terror organizations keep trying to come up with new ways to strike. In 1987, for example, a terrorist succeeded in penetrating the northern border from Lebanon by flying in a small motorized glider. But before getting to any civilian, he was killed by Israeli soldiers. From then on, the Israeli army and air force have been on the watch not only for jets, planes, and even hot-air balloons (used during an earlier, failed attempt) but gliders as well. In fact, this is the pattern of the war against terrorism – to learn the lessons of previous attacks, and to adapt and improvise in order to prevent them from ever happening again.

Another more recent, and more frightening, case in point was in 1989, when a Palestinian terrorist from the Gaza Strip, riding as a passenger on the Tel Aviv to Jerusalem bus, suddenly pounced on the wheel and sent the vehicle plummeting down a gorge. Sixteen people were killed and scores injured in that tragedy. Since then, special guard rails protecting the driver have been installed in buses to prevent any such future attempt.

I remember well how the first days after they were installed, people would look at them with a sense of worry, even with a trace of fear on their faces. This, after all, is what terrorism is really about

– to terrorize. But for the Israelis, those traces quickly vanished. Within days, people were not even giving the added security measure a second glance, much less a second thought.

All Israelis are Soldiers

Long after the war against terror remains a subject solely for history books and historians, the Israeli view of terrorism will still be an integral part of the national mentality.

At the height of the world terrorist wave in the 1970s, when governments were releasing captured terrorists right and left according to their latest demands, Israel made it clear that it would not only never negotiate with terrorists, but Israeli civilians who find themselves under attack should remember the cardinal rule: that as far as terrorism is concerned, all civilians are soldiers. More than just a saying, this has become an effective psychological weapon which has succeeded in regaining the initiative in the battle against terror.

Israelis prefer to think of themselves as soldiers in the war against terrorism because soldiers, unlike victims, have the ability to fight back, and even win. This very point came up in a strikingly different context during the Gulf War. In the midst of the Scud missile attacks on Tel Aviv, when Saddam Hussein was asked why he was bombing Israeli civilians, he replied that in Israel, "everyone was a soldier."

LIVING WITH TERRORISM

After scaring you considerably, the time has come again to put things in their proper perspective. It's important to keep in mind that a far more appropriate title for this section, instead of "Living with Terrorism," should have been the more truthful but far too lengthy "Living with the Minimally Few Precautions Necessary in View of the Extremely Remote Possibility of Terrorism."

On a day-to-day basis, what living with terrorism really comes

The Police Bomb Squad going on yet another mission.

down to is merely taking notice of what people in other countries would see as some rather disturbing goings-on. The classic example is the famous Israeli police sapper.

The Bomb Squad

Anyone who spends any time here is bound to witness what in Israel is commonplace occurrence: a street will be temporarily blocked off or a bus station evacuated, because someone has noticed "a suspicious object." This can be anything from a suitcase to a bag or package that has been lost or forgotten by its owner.

Security awareness is so high in Israel that this happens all the time, many times a day in the big cities. It's a familiar routine. The police are immediately called in, the site is evacuated, passers-by are instructed not to approach, and within minutes the police bomb squad arrives.

Explosive Diapers.

Very busy men indeed, these bomb squad sappers. I always get a kick out of never having seen a police sapper who was not a religious Jew, going about their jobs wearing the traditional head covering. Then again, with this job, it's not hard to understand why!

In any event, the sapper goes about his routine job, using the special robot which has been invented for this purpose. And taking no chances whatsoever, he explodes a small charge next to the suspicious object in order to set off any possible bomb.

Ninety-nine percent of the time, it's someone's forgotten laundry or groceries that gets blown up. I have even seen what turned out to be a package of diapers explode, and in another unforgettable incident, a box full of feathers, which flew into the sky for half a city block.

To the Israeli pedestrians and bus passengers who are waiting to get on with their business, this is an everyday delay, in no way out of the ordinary. On their faces you often see impatience, and sometimes even mild curiosity. But the one thing you very rarely see is fear.

On the Buses

Bus travel in Israel is another example of where security awareness has become a way of life.

When riding the buses, Israelis are used to looking around their seats and taking note of whether there is a bag or package without an apparent owner and, if there is, not hesitating to tell the driver about it.

And it's part of the driver's job to search the vehicle thoroughly before allowing passengers to board; he or she is responsible not only for driving the bus but for security as well.

I remember one typical bus ride in Tel Aviv when a woman noticed on the luggage rack above her seat a blue canvas bag. She calmly asked the passengers around her if the bag belonged to any of them. Negative responses came from all sides.

137

She then called out to the whole bus: "To whom does this bag belong?" No answer.

Nobody at this stage was nervous or even beginning to get nervous, but here and there you could tell that some people were beginning to think about it.

Once again the woman, this time with a bit more urgency in her voice, asked: "Whose bag is this?" After a long pause, a leathery old guy, looking like a veteran of every major battle since the 1948 War of Independence, audibly sighed and growled from his seat: "Yes, yes, it's my bag." For all his annoyance, and despite the evident war experience which was written all over his face, the lady did not hesitate to bawl him out for not speaking up sooner, and for not putting the bag above his seat where it belonged.

All living with terrorism really amounts to is getting used to such incidents and facing them calmly, and even with a sense of humor, if possible. It's a largely passive role, the best example of which is the typical "suspicious object" episode, where your only job is simply to stand behind the police barricade and wait for the sapper to finish his work. Your most important task is psychological – to neither let yourself nor your imagination be disturbed by what in the vast majority of countries would be a disturbing event. Such is the Israeli way of life.

The only time your security role becomes in any way active is when traveling across the Green Line into the Territories.

THE TERRITORIES

In Israel, geography not only plays an essential role in history, politics, and religion but in security as well. For example, it's important for those intent on visiting Christian sites to know that there should be a world of difference between their level of security awareness during a visit to, for example, Bethlehem and to Nazareth. Why? Geography is the answer. Nazareth is located in Israel proper, while Bethlehem is in the Territories.

The Intifada

A traveler crossing the Green Line goes from an area with a friendly population to an area occupied under military rule, with a population hostile to Israelis and, in some cases, tourists as well.

The security situation in the Territories worsened considerably at the end of 1987, when the Palestinian uprising, or *Intifada*, broke out with massive rioting and stone throwing. Although the once large-scale riots which marked the uprising in its first year have by and large come to an end, the *Intifada* goes on, and stone throwing is still a daily experience.

As far as travel in the Territories goes, one of the biggest hazards is simply driving around, because Israeli cars are often the targets of stone-throwing youths. The *Intifada* has in many ways turned into a license plate war – this due to the fact that in Israel proper, all cars have yellow plates, while in the Territories, all the license plates are blue.

Consequently, a car with yellow license plates in the Gaza Strip, Nablus, Hebron, Ramallah, Jericho or Bethlehem most likely means that its driver is Israeli and, according to the fighting code of the Palestinian youths, probably a Jewish settler. It can thus attract stones like a magnet. For this reason alone, a leisurely Saturday afternoon drive in the Territories is definitely not recommended.

The Six Day War Mentality

Watch out especially for what is known as the "Six Day War Mentality." Common especially among Israelis of the older generation, it usually goes something like this: "Of course it's safe to travel in the Territories. In any event, what difference does it make? We won the battles, it's our land, and it's important to travel freely – with your head held high – everywhere in Israel, no matter which side of the Green Line you're on."

Before the *Intifada*, I would have had to convince the reader, as in the earlier passage about the merits of not traveling to Israel via

Egypt or Jordan, the advantages of being more conservative. But with the long-lasting Palestinian uprising, even many of the old-time Israelis who once held their heads high in the Territories have found themselves lowering them quickly and running for cover.

It was not always like this. At one time, many Israelis would routinely travel in the Territories, sometimes touring or hiking, and other times hunting for bargains in the Arab markets. It was common for many Jerusalem residents to do their weekly shopping in Bethlehem on Saturdays, when all the stores in the capital were closed. Hundreds of Tel Aviv residents used to cross the Green Line into the Arab city of Kalkilya every Saturday to grab a bargain at the famous open-air markets. But unfortunately, all that came to an end with the *Intifada*.

To this day, years after the uprising began, Kalkilya remains virtually a ghost town on Saturday; and that wonderful Bethlehem grocery store that I used to shop in (which had more imported food than any Israeli store) has long since closed down.

For all the marginal political gains the Palestinians have managed to achieve with the *Intifada*, and for all the loss of life and limb, what has been truly catastrophic is the damage to the economy of the Territories, and to the standard of living of its residents.

BE AWARE

The final word in this chapter on security has to be awareness. Just as you would not take a walk in any major city on the planet without a certain degree of awareness, so too in Israel should this be the standard rule of conduct.

Whether shopping in Tel Aviv, dining out in Haifa, or even strolling through the streets of Jerusalem's Old City, all that is demanded is a minimal degree of watchfulness which to most city dwellers is already second nature. That's it. Those accustomed to the daily headlines depicting Israel as some sort of combat zone will no doubt be relieved to learn that this is all you need to know.

TIPS ON SECURITY

- Israelis are obligated by law to carry their identity cards with them at all times. Correspondingly, visitors in Israel are advised to always keep their passports at hand.
- For those who decide to fly with El Al, there is one way to avoid most of the time-consuming security procedures. In several cities around the world, El Al offers a pre-flight service, where you can check in your bags the night before your flight, go through the security in a relatively comfortable, quick, and pressure-free atmosphere, and even receive your boarding pass in advance. This enables you to proceed directly to the flight gate upon arriving at the airport.
- For those intent on traveling to Israel via the Egyptian or Jordanian overland routes, a few points to keep in mind. At Taba (near Eilat) and at Rafiah (the border post between Egypt and Israel on the southern tip of the Gaza Strip), there can sometimes be long waits. This also holds true for the Allenby Bridge, which serves as the border crossing between Israel and Jordan over the Jordan River.
- Another important point to remember about traveling from Jordan is that it's forbidden for private vehicles to cross the Allenby Bridge into Israel, so forget about renting a car in Amman and driving it here.
- Travelers intent on touring the Territories are advised to take one of the many organized tours, which are much safer than traveling alone. For those especially adventurous souls, tours of Palestinian refugee camps in the Territories can be arranged through the United Nations in Jerusalem.

- Christmas Eve in Bethlehem is an event which should not be missed, especially by Christian visitors who wish to take part in the famous Midnight Mass. As far as security is concerned, this is one case where traveling in the Territories is completely safe. The Israeli Army goes to unprecedented lengths to ensure the safety of all those participating in the festivities, which each year brings thousands of people. Security instructions and special travel arrangements are advertised well in advance.

Chapter Eight

THE MEDIA

Beeep!![6]
KOL YISRAEL.

Seu.

...ssrr... crackle... clack... rrrzz...drzzr....

"Rabbi Dr Immanuel Jakobovits … replied that modern science and technology had done so much to undermine religion that it was time they were used to serve it."

—Colin Cross, *What is Judaism?*

GLOBAL NETWORK

This chapter is partly irrelevant. Israel, like other developed countries, is a full-fledged member of the global communications revolution; one more neighborhood in the modern "world city," with television cable channels of New York and Hong Kong financial markets, Russian ballet, European Cup football (soccer to Americans), and NBA basketball.

There is radio from the BBC World Service, the Voice of America, and even Radio Moscow (which broadcasts to Israel in Hebrew as well as in English). And of course there are the newspapers, where everything from *USA Today* and *The Wall Street Journal* to *The Guardian* and *Le Soir* are available.

But in a country where the news is central to everyday life, there are some unique aspects of the media. Israeli television, radio, and the written press are fascinating not only because they represent the nation's "popular culture," but because they are also a reflection, a mirror even, of the country itself – of its people and its personality. Above all, a look at the media provides the litmus test to two paramount political questions: Is the nation democratic? And is it an informed democracy?

TELEVISION

The year 1967 was a watershed year in Israel, not only because of the Six Day War and the beginning of the problems of the Territories, but because it was the year that television came to Israel.

Since then, there have been some strange and unique programs broadcast on Israeli television: From the trial of Nazi war criminal John Demjanjuk (allegedly known during World War II as Ivan the Terrible) to the live broadcast at the height of the 1990 election, when ultraorthodox Jewish groups gathered to hear their 92-year-old spiritual leader decree in Yiddish which party he would support to form the next government. He chose instead to scold people about eating pork.

The whole world on sale each morning. The variety of newspapers on sale include "The European," "USA Today," "Le Figaro" and "The International Herald Tribune."

For the most part, Israel Television broadcasts on only one channel. This alone is enough to cause considerable culture shock to those accustomed to spending their spare time scanning the multitude of television channels usually available to them. In Israel, this one channel is divided three ways: educational programs during the day, programs in Arabic in the early evening, and Hebrew news and general entertainment at night.

Israel Television's educational programs, which are broadcast from the morning hours until 5 p.m., include everything from the truly educational Israeli version of *Sesame Street* (which like the original is fun and entertaining, but it is in Hebrew instead) to the imported cartoons and children's adventure films which only with some difficulty can be called educational.

It's with these imported programs from Europe, Australia, Canada and the United States that Israeli kids from an early age begin training themselves in the task so central to Israeli television viewing: getting used to reading the Hebrew subtitles which appear at the bottom of the screen.

The Joys of Non-Dubbing

In Israel, there is very little dubbing, whether it be a French film, a BBC documentary, or the latest speech by Mikhail Gorbachev on the nightly news.

Israelis hear the original language and look to the bottom of the screen for the translation. It's quite funny to see what in Israel is a familiar scene: a family relaxing in front of the tube, with the younger children sitting on the edge of their seats because they are straining to read the subtitles.

As I have found out as a newcomer to the Hebrew language, those translated sentences move awfully fast across the bottom of the screen. So, together with the kids, I too strain (and unlike them, curse if the next subtitle appears before I have managed to finish reading the last one).

Arabic Programs

It comes as a surprise to many that Israel Television broadcasts exclusively in Arabic some two hours in the early evening. The nation thus dedicates a portion of its television to its Arabic-speaking citizens – the Israeli Arabs, Bedouins, Druze and Circassians. The reason why is not purely altruistic, however, because the programming is not only targeted to this audience, but also to Arabs in the Territories, and even those living in Arab countries across Israel's borders. The electronic media knows no national boundary, and one of the strange things about the Middle East is that enemy countries not only send their sons and daughters to fight each other, but also to watch each other's television programs.

The nation's Jewish citizens are also keen viewers of Arabic programs on Israel Television. Comprehension is no problem (even

147

though many Israelis do understand Arabic) because, as with French or English programs, there is always the Hebrew translation.

In fact, what has become a tradition for the entire country is the famous weekly Arabic film, which is broadcast early Friday evening. Like country songs with the same theme repeated over and over again – lost love – these classic movies from all over the Middle East weave complex romantic plots which make American soap operas look simple by comparison. And like the soap operas, they are just as eagerly watched by an addicted audience. In a country as torn by Arab-Israeli strife as this, such exchanges of popular culture help contribute to fighting racism and hatred, and to keeping coexistence alive.

Prime Time Israel

But it's in the evening, from 8 p.m. to be exact, that Israel Television puts forth its biggest effort. This part of the programming is called "general" television (in contrast to educational or Arabic television), and general is not a bad word to describe the wide variety of programs.

The good with the bad, it includes many of the top-rated hits of previous years on American networks: *Dallas* and *Dynasty* were extremely popular, as was *The Cosby Show* (which was so successful that Bill Cosby's books have even been translated into Hebrew).

Also on the menu are documentaries, drama, adventure, and comedy programs from BBC, Canadian, and Australian television; musical features with video clips that are so popular abroad; and the all-important twice-weekly films, which are very rarely Israeli, sometimes French, but for the most part usually the best pickings from Hollywood.

The Friday night movie in particular is often an excellent one, and possibly because the religious are not among the television audience during the Sabbath, movies are uncensored!

So for the selective foreign, immigrant or expat viewer, Israel

Television offers some good entertainment. But the best news of all is that when your all-time favorite movie is shown on Wednesday or Friday night, or a favorite comedy or drama series finds its way to Israel, the one thing that won't disturb your viewing pleasure is commercials. On Israel Television, there are none!

Hebrew Programming

However, if the media is a reflection of the nation, then the most important part of television is without doubt the Hebrew programming.

Hebrew films, dramas, comedies, musical performances and political satire, all expressions of the Israeli culture, are the most popular programs. As one might expect in a country so intensely focused on the news, a high percentage of broadcasting time is devoted to what is called "actuality" – news, interviews, documentaries and talk shows all dealing with the current events and issues of the day.

Among the seemingly infinite number of Hebrew programs over the years, there have been a few which made such a significant impact that they deserve to be called historic.

When extremist Meir Kahane arrived in the country from the United States and began disseminating racist propaganda, Israel Television screened a documentary entitled *The Prophet of Hate*. A shocking profile of Kahane and his ideologies, it left a deep impression, and in many ways led to the public campaign which culminated in the Knesset law against racism.

Another important and ambitious documentary was the *Pillar of Fire*. This extraordinary series took five years to produce and had documented interviews and film footage of the history of the country from 1896 to 1948. Shown over 19 parts in the spring and summer of 1981 (proving that when the subject is right, there are no limits to the length of programs), *Pillar of Fire* did more to educate Israel's youth than any formal history course.

An Israeli and his "tube."

And when the recent wave of Russian immigration began to rock the country, Israel Television sent their top journalist to the Soviet Union to tour the republics and seek out the many Jewish communities, while investigating anti-Semitism. The result was very impressive: an eight-part series which was the talk of the country for two months. During one episode, a member of the anti-Semitic Soviet party, "Pamyat," explained why he wanted to get rid of Jews. That interview did more to increase Israeli understanding (and sympathy) for the absorption of Russian Jews than any government publicity campaign.

Mad for News
The heart of Israel Television is its nightly news.

When 9 p.m. rolls around each night, the vast majority of Israelis sit themselves in front of the tube and wait for the latest bad news.

Depending on just how bad the day was, the news can go on for half an hour, 45 minutes, or even an hour or more.

The good news at the time of writing is that Israel Radio is planning to simultaneously translate this nightly broadcast into English. This means that you can watch the news on television, turn down the volume, and listen to the translation on radio instead.

When a big event hits the country, whether it be a terrorist attack or a major political development, the television becomes the standard bearer of the nation's worry, fear or excitement.

One of the most memorable news reports was a special Friday evening program which summed up the events of the past week. It had been a particularly bad week, with two terrorist attacks and the subsequent angry reaction of the Jewish people. Thus the tone of the news seemed to be even more apocalyptic than usual.

The newscaster that night chose to end the doomsday reports with a filmed interview of an elderly Israeli-Arab farmer. A wise old man who talked about all the hate and violence he had seen during his years in the Middle East, from the time of Turkish and British rule to the current era, he described how he was still optimistic that peace would eventually come.

In a masterpiece of a documentary, the interview was conducted as the farmer pruned his beautifully kept vineyard. The camera kept switching back and forth from his seamed and kindly face to his gnarled old hands as he went about his work, cutting off the dead branches and lovingly shaping the live ones. Like poetry, this timely report soothed and calmed the taut nerves of an entire nation after an extremely rough week.

OTHER CHANNELS

In recent years, another channel has been added to Israel Television. It is called, with novel originality, The Second Channel. However, it only broadcasts on a limited basis, is difficult to receive in many parts of the country, and even requires a special antenna or cable to pick up in the Tel Aviv area. But for those who do succeed in hooking onto this network, The Second Channel offers some good choices of television viewing, especially for the foreign resident. A lot of good films, international sports programs, and US news programs like *CNN*, *Nightline* and *The McNeil-Lehrer Report* are shown.

But one of the most interesting aspects of being a television viewer in Israel is having the opportunity to see what the programs broadcast by neighboring Jordan and Syria are like.

Jordanian TV

Jordanian television's nightly news in English, for example, is highly unusual as far as news is concerned. There seems to be a set formula for broadcasting news.

On Jordanian TV, no matter what the top story of the day is, the opening report always starts off with something about King Hussein and his family. These stories have opened the news on days when Jordan was making world headlines, whether because of its support for Iraq during the Gulf War, or an attack on Israel. For years, this was the only televised English news available in Israel. But in 1990, Israel Television finally got its act together and began broadcasting a 15-minute news bulletin in English every evening.

Besides this, Jordanian television is also an occasional viewer's choice because one of its two channels is devoted entirely to programs in English and French.

Called "the foreign channel," it offers some high quality drek from the United States and France – movies, documentaries, and comedy or adventure imports, all sold on the thriving international television market. In addition to the news program in English, there is also one in French. So if you prefer getting your daily dose in French, enjoy. And speaking of this, one of the strangest things on Jordanian television is a news bulletin in, believe it or not, Hebrew. Israel and Jordan are still in a state of war, so apparently King

Hussein remains interested in the information as well as the weapons war.

Syrian TV

A real view of a nation at war is provided when tuning in to Syrian television. There is really very little to tune in for, as all broadcasts are in Arabic, and appear to be limited to political speeches, patriotic songs, and Islamic sermons.

However, one particular telecast that was interesting enough to be shown in excerpts on Israel Television was a special induction ceremony of Syrian soldiers. What was special about it was that the inductees, both men and women, showed their love for Syria in great fanfare by eating snakes – live snakes. As they say in Hebrew, "Bete Avone" (Good Appetite)!

Middle East TV

The last choice for the television viewer is a South Lebanese channel called *Middle East TV*. But it's not really Lebanese television; only the broadcast transmitter is in South Lebanon.

On this channel, the pick of American programs is poor, but its redeeming feature is the American football and baseball games which are televised from time to time.

The station is owned by Christian broadcasters from the United States (the same ones who televise *The 700 Club*, which is broadcast every night, along with a myriad of Christian programs). For those who don't live in the north of the country (Haifa and northward), it is difficult to receive this channel, unless you have a special antenna or cable.

Cable TV and Video

Finally, there's always the possibility of leaving the region entirely by subscribing to cable television. A multitude of cable services are available in Israel, and one can gain access to channels from all over the world. For those who see no possibility whatsoever of enjoying television, it's important to note that video is also very popular here. Every city in the country, and even most of the small towns, have video stores with a large selection of movies. This includes (Holy Land or not, ultraorthodox or not) a large assortment of adult films.

RADIO

Radio is very special in Israel. The exceptionally high percentage of radio listeners sometimes causes you to think that Israel is somehow still in the 1940s, during the pre-TV era. In how many countries does the bus driver automatically turn up the volume of the radio – every hour on the hour – so that all the passengers can hear the news broadcast? Every hour you will hear the six-beep time signal of *Kol Yisrael* ("the Voice of Israel") and notice people prick up their ears, take a deep breath, and wait for the latest news.

If there is one thing that symbolizes the fast pace of Israeli life, it's these hourly news bulletins preceded by their beeps. Israelis about to depart for their yearly vacation will tell you that the single most important thing they need to get away from are "those damn beeps." And, God forbid, if another war breaks out during your stay, you will see another strange sight: Israelis walking down the streets holding a transistor radio to an ear, as if it were glued there. It's a scene you will see only in countries where news is a vital part of everyday life.

The Second Network

Israel Radio's major news station, called *Reshet Bet* or "the second network," is a good example of just how important news is to the people.

Over the years as the most popular of all the radio stations, *Reshet Bet* employs some of Israel's finest journalists. In addition to the hourly bulletins, which usually average about four minutes, the station also broadcasts news headlines on the half-hour, and lengthy news journals can be heard in the morning, afternoon, evening, and even at midnight.

In between, amidst occasional music, there are even more news programs, whether they be interviews and talk shows, programs on economic and international news, or documentaries. All this goes without mentioning the special bulletins which can, and often do, interrupt the regular programming at any time. The result is not only an informed audience, but a people who find themselves inundated with news to the point of obsession.

The Military Radio

Another big news outlet is the army radio station called *Galei Tzhal*, or "the Israel Defense Force Frequency." For the reader unfamiliar with Israel, the term "military radio" brings to mind all sorts of negative connotations. This, after all, is the name of the station which announces the latest military coup, the suspension of elections, the nightly curfew and the new wave of arrests. In fact the military radio has the opposite effect; it provides an additional independent source of news.

With its core of professional journalists, most of *Galei Tzhal*'s broadcasters are young soldiers – men and women who do their regular army service not in the infantry or the air force, but on the radio. Like *Reshet Bet*, the IDF radio also broadcasts four in-depth news programs a day; and every hour (on the half-hour), it presents its own separate news bulletin.

In addition to news, IDF radio also offers some excellent music, especially the jazz and rock variety. And for those insomniacs among the readers, it broadcasts some of its best music in the middle of the night.

The Third Network

For the rock and rollers, Israel Radio provides *Reshet Gimmel*, "the third network." When I first came to Israel, I remembered how it

155

supplied me with my first bit of successful Hebrew comprehension. Having just learned that the Hebrew word for "the" is *ha*, I got a big kick out of hearing the announcer identify one of my favorite groups, The Kinks, as "HaKinks." Luckily, he decided not to translate into Hebrew the word kinks.

The Voice of Music

As I grew older, I moved away from HaKinks to HaClassical. If this is your taste as well, then you have come to the right country. One of Israel's radio stations is called *Kol HaMusica* ("the Voice of Music"). With a minimum of talk and, most importantly, no commercials whatsoever, it offers 18 hours of classical music on FM stereo every day. Take a walk through Israeli neighborhoods and you'll hear its luscious sounds flowing out of windows into the streets.

The First Network

Without a doubt the most remarkable radio station is *Reshet Alef*, "the first network." Here is a living example of what the state of Israel is all about: a land of, and for, immigrants.

Reshet Alef broadcasts news programs in no less than 12 different languages – English, French, Spanish and Yiddish among them. When I first arrived, my news came from the station's English service, which provides a 15-minute news bulletin three times a day, at 7 a.m, 1 p.m., and 8 p.m.

With the current wave of Russian immigration, it became clear that one network alone was not enough to provide the needs for these thousands of new immigrants. So Israel Radio started yet another station, which broadcast all day long in Russian.

The Fourth Network

Israel Radio's Arabic station is *Reshet Daled*, or "the fourth network." Broadcasting a wide range of programs, including three hour-long news journals each day, this station has become one of the most popular and influential sources of news in the entire Middle East. And in contrast to Israel Television, which is received only in bordering countries, Israel Radio's Arabic service is picked up as far away as Iraq, Saudi Arabia and Yemen.

The Fifth Network (the Voice of Israel)

Rounding out the list of Israel Radio stations is *Reshet Hey*, "the fifth network." This is the overseas service which broadcasts around the world in 15 different languages on shortwave. Wherever a Jewish community is to be found, the Voice of Israel radio can be heard. If you own a radio which has shortwave, a good way to prepare for your trip to Israel is to tune in to the news and feature programs offered in English, or in another language of your choice.

The Voice of Peace

Another option available to local listeners is the station called the *Voice of Peace*. Offering lots of good music, from classical to rock, this privately owned station broadcasts from, of all places, a ship in the Mediterranean Sea.

The most memorable thing about the *Voice of Peace* is its opening call signal, which is heard every hour on the hour before and after the Hebrew news. Beginning with an excerpt from Menachem Begin's famous speech at the signing of the peace treaty with Egypt, one hears him emotionally declare in his accented English: "No more war, no more bloodshed." Then the stirring *Voice of Peace* music comes surging in, followed by the dramatic announcement: "From somewhere in the Mediterranean, this is the *Voice of Peace*." An opening more suited to the coming of the Messiah than to musical programs, no? But even then, this is the right country for it!

The station is owned by an Israeli, Abie Nathan. One of the country's original peace demonstrators, in 1966 Nathan went as far as to fly his own plane to Cairo to try and convince the Egyptian government to make peace with Israel. Since returning from that famous flight, Nathan has remained one of the most consistently vocal voices in the peace movement. In any event, it's recommended to tune in to the *Voice of Peace* when in Israel – if not for its music, then for that great opening call signal.

Foreign Frequencies

Finally, as with television, for those who find nothing interesting on the local radio, there's always the possibility of leaving the region entirely by tuning in to foreign stations.

The BBC, the Voice of America, Radio Monte Carlo from France, and even Radio Moscow can be picked up quite easily in Israel – not on shortwave, but on your regular AM dial. During the Gulf War, many Israelis chose to increase their sources of news by listening to these stations as well as Israel Radio.

For the BBC, perhaps its most famous day in Israel came during Yom Kippur in 1982. Menachem Begin claimed in a government investigation that he first heard about the infamous Beirut Sabra and Shatila massacres through the British station, while the Israeli stations were off the air because of the holiday.

NEWSPAPERS

Israel has more national newspapers than any other country in the world. There are some 26 dailies, 18 of which are published in other languages besides Hebrew.

There are nine different newspapers in Russian alone, and with the thousands of Russian Jews flooding the country lately, even the nation's top selling newspaper, *Yediot Achronot* ("The Latest News"), now includes a news supplement in Russian.

This media deluge is not confined to the immigrant alone. The average Israeli has a pick of everything from high quality intellectual journals to the Hebrew version of *The National Enquirer*. It

Israelis are always hungry for the latest news.

seems as if everyone has his or her own personal newspaper – from the old-timer who still prefers to read the news in Yiddish, to the young Israeli who buys the newspaper most closely identified with his or her political views.

For the English speaker, there is no question about which newspaper to buy. At the moment, *The Jerusalem Post* is the only English daily in the country. With a long tradition going back well before the founding of the state (when it was known as *The Palestine Post*), it has had its share of ups and downs over the years. Though still not taken completely seriously by Israeli politicians, it has a very loyal following, and in recent years has moved to the political right, away from its traditional liberal stand.

Political Party Preference Papers

The link between the media and politics is nowhere more apparent than in the nation's press. Many newspapers are politically aligned, and some are even official party organs.

The Labor Party, for example, has its own paper, as does the socialist Mapam Party, the National Religious Party and the ultra-orthodox Agudat Yisrael Party. Many of the newspapers that are not formally aligned, however, do not hesitate to make their political preferences clear.

The two major afternoon dailies, *Ma'ariv* ("Evening") and *Yediot Achronot*, differ not only in format, but in political orientation. *Ma'ariv* is much more supportive of the Likud and its philosophy, while *Yediot* takes a more critical line consistent with the Labor Party.

The elite of the Hebrew press is the daily *HaAretz* ("The Nation"). The most prestigious and most expensive of Israel's newspapers, *HaAretz* employs some of the best journalists in the country, and has many of the biggest scoops in the history of Israeli journalism to its credit. Israel's most respected military commentator, Ze'ev Schiff, writes for the paper. Especially in times of crisis, his articles have great impact not only on the public, but on the political and defense establishment as well. For example, immediately following the Gulf War, Schiff caused a sensation when he published a story charging that many of the gas masks issued in Israel were defective. The subsequent uproar led to a government investigation.

The editorial page of *HaAretz* is one of the most scrutinized pieces of journalism, especially by the nation's politicians. Often critical, sometimes scathing, and above all fiercely independent, this newspaper has contributed much over the years to keeping Israeli politics, and politicians, in line.

Chapter Nine

DOING BUSINESS

The "in"-look in Israel.

"False scales are an abomination to the Lord, but accurate weights win his favor."

—Proverbs 11:1

THE TROUBLE WITH BUSINESS

"What's the only way to make a small fortune in Israel? Arrive here with a big fortune."

This, the favorite joke of the Israeli businessman and businesswoman, gives but a hint of the difficulties which doing business in Israel can pose for both the native resident and foreigner.

On a day-to-day basis, this could indeed be the single toughest and most frustrating aspect of the Israeli way of life. And it's not only because of Israel's astronomical taxes, among the highest in the world.

The periods of runaway inflation, frequent devaluation of the national currency, the financial uncertainty that accompanies it all, or even the wars which can put a stop to the entire country, are all contributors. But with all the up-to-date conveniences of modern business – the computers, the facsimile systems, the mobile telephones – a big part of what makes doing business in Israel such an uphill battle is the unique character of the Israeli businessmen and businesswomen themselves.

The Merry-Go-Round Bureaucracy

Here's one typical example: After much hard work, you finally succeeded in tracking down all the offices, officers, bureaus and bureaucrats needed for approving your business transaction. Some were in the reserves, some were on vacation, some were on sick leave, and some simply weren't. But you got the job done.

However, before resting easy, your quickly budding Israeli instincts tell you to make one last, seemingly unnecessary phone call to the office of the head bureaucrat to confirm that the whole process has indeed been done correctly.

To your great chagrin (but not to your great surprise – why, after all, did you make this phone call), the aforementioned bureaucrat informs you that "the procedures have just been changed," and you now have to start all over again.

The Free Blood Pressure Exercise

Here's another one: Not yet accustomed to the Israeli way of doing business, you schedule an all-important meeting for 2 p.m. in your office. Unbelievably, your man or woman does not show up at a quarter to two, at ten to two, or even at five minutes to two.

At 2 p.m. sharp – nothing. Not even a phone call to apologize, explain the delay, or arrange a new time for another meeting (only a phone call from a hospital emergency room could in your mind possibly, but not quite, justify such behavior). Sin. Crime. Outrage. A violation of all the standards of business conduct and professionalism which you have had drilled into you since Day 1.

At a quarter past two, at half past two, at a quarter to three, you are still waiting. Then at 3 p.m., after you have already decided not only to cancel the deal but are mad enough to have him or her killed (the only question remaining is whether or not to do it slowly), he or she shows up, hurries into the office looking hassled and harried, and, incredibly enough, offers no excuse. Not a traffic accident, not an illness, not a sudden death in the family, nothing. There is no mention whatsoever that he or she is an hour late.

As if very little has happened (and to the average businessman or businesswoman in Israel, very little has), the meeting goes on, and your education in Israeli business practices, along with your blood pressure, continues to increase.

One Strike and You're Out!

Or this: At the peak of a typical work day, your computer, along with the rest of the electricity in the office, suddenly shuts down, jettisoning the vital program you were so frantically trying to finish on time into the irretrievable blackness of the computer void.

"What the hell is going on?" you ask your Israeli secretary, with not a little annoyance.

"Oh," she replies nonchalantly, "the electrical workers are on strike again."

Strikes, an almost daily occurrence in Israel, could affect everything from the bank, the airport, the phones, the radios and televisions and, yes, even the medical services. One of the longest strikes in Israeli history was, believe it or not, by the nation's doctors.

The guiding principle of the powerful Israeli labor unions happens to also hold true for the country's entire business community. There are no limits, boundaries, ethics or rules; all is fair in the rough and tumble, maddening, and often Kafkaesque world of Israeli business.

THE BUREAUCRACY

From ordinary clerks, administrators and civil servants to the political appointees who make up Israel's massive bureaucracy, the Hebrew word which describes them all is *pakid*.

Israel's most influential columnist, Yoel Marcus of *HaAretz*,

165

attempted to explain the often insurmountable problems of doing business in Israel by commenting that "somewhere between the countries of Afghanistan and Pakistan is located a nation called Pakidistan, where in order to get anything done, you have to slog your way through the muddy quagmire of official bureaucracy."

Capable of killing many a deal in Israel, this vast network of employees has somehow come to hold unprecedented power. How did this monster get created? The answer lies in Israel's history.

History of Israeli Bureaucracy

Many of the institutions which make up the backbone of the Israeli bureaucracy were formed even before the state came into existence in 1948. During the years of the British mandate, the Jewish community of Palestine was allowed to enjoy a considerable degree of autonomy, with the exception of political and military authority.

Much of the energy of the idealistic Zionist settlers went into this autonomy – into the formation of economic and social institutions, health and educational bodies, and voluntary and civic organizations.

The movement, known as Labor Zionism (the predecessor of today's Labor Party), made great progress in forming trade unions along with other political, economic, and social organizations. Their single most impressive accomplishment was what became known as "the Histadrut" (the Israel Labor Federation), which brought all these different bodies together under one roof and, in the best tradition of Russian socialism, under their own party control. Accumulating vast economic power (and vast bureaucracies), these organizations not only provided the institutional framework for the new state, but became the model for later Israeli government ministries after 1948.

The Problems of Israeli Bureaucracy

However, there are other factors which to this day still contribute to the malignant growth of Israeli bureaucracy. Politicians, political pressures, and indeed the entire political structure of the nation are mostly to blame. Not only do political appointees make up the senior levels of the country's bureaucracies, but political pressures have even led to the creation of new ones.

A good example was the election crisis of 1990, when both the Labor and Likud parties were promising ministries, money, and power to the small fringe parties (most of them ultraorthodox) in exchange for support. One of the results of the Likud victory was that it ran out of ministries to parcel out to its many coalition partners. What to do? No problem, because in the Israeli system of government the most important consideration is political party support; all else is secondary. The answer? Create a new ministry, of course. The result: the latest ministry, at the time of writing, is the Ministry of Jerusalem Affairs.

Besides the vast funds taken from the empty coffers of the national treasury in order to establish, build, and man this new ministry – including offices, cars, and other perks for its staff – the Jerusalem business community, along with potential investors, found themselves with something they did not need – yet another bureaucracy barring the way to doing successful and efficient business.

Protection

Is there some secret to dealing with this vast labyrinthine body known as Pakidistan? There is no magic key that will open all doors to successful business, but one of the methods (perhaps the only one) which will usually help is something known in anglicized Hebrew-Yiddish as *protektzia*.

The word is not a reference to some Mafioso secret deal, blackmail, or influence peddling, but merely an older, more Middle Eastern way of doing business. More talk than action, it focuses less on professionalism and more on knowing people, personal contacts, and personal dealings.

One of the centers of the Israeli business bureaucracy – the Ministry of Trade and Industry.

THE PERSONAL TOUCH

Getting to know the bureaucrat by his or her first name could well be the most important step in learning the ropes of doing successful business in Israel. And it's not only a matter of the informality of first names; spending an hour or two chatting him or her up over a cup of coffee is also a vital part of the game. (To the Israeli public servant on a fixed monthly salary, time is definitely not money.)

Such behavior is recommended not only because it often helps to get what you need, whether it be bureaucratic approval or assistance, but also because it's one way to achieve the all-important "in" – the most essential word in the Israeli business vocabulary.

In Israel's small financial community, getting to know people is vital, and the bureaucrat can help. Indeed, their offices have become the watering holes of Israeli commerce.

One of the positive aspects of doing business here is that such an "in" is relatively easy to achieve. The Israeli business community is not snobbishly closed to outsiders as in other countries, and with relatively little effort the newcomer can find himself or herself on the inside.

The flip side of the coin is far less encouraging. Those who remain on the outside, whether due to unfamiliarity with the Israelis or inability to cope with the Israeli style, find doing business a near impossible task.

The Flexible Israeli

It should also be kept in mind that another factor contributing to the importance of the personal touch is, for want of a better word, the "flexibility" of the Israeli way of doing business. Here, every bureaucrat has the power to change, amend, and even ignore rules and regulations which in other countries would be black and white matters of the law.

The shortcut is without question one of the most well-established facts of Israeli economic life, and getting to know the people

169

who can help you find it is one of the most important areas of *protektzia.*

This will undoubtedly irritate those used to doing things straight by the book. In the zigzag world of business in Israel, everybody seemingly writes his or her own.

Informality

Israeli business is conducted very informally. Spectacular offices, big expense accounts, and long executive lunches are not part of business. Those used to such standards will certainly find Israeli offices dumpy, Israeli lunches short, and Israeli expense accounts virtually nonexistent.

However, there are advantages to the Israeli style. There is much less emphasis here on status, ranking and titles. Here, the "deputy to the assistant general manager" is not treated with slightly less respect than his or her boss, the assistant general manager.

And as far as the exalted general manager is concerned, another advantage of the Israeli way of doing business is that he or she is far more accessible than those in other countries. And all the nonsense of "treating executives with the respect befitting their office" does not exist.

On a Personal Basis

Indeed, one of my favorite things about the Israeli way of doing business is this marked lack of stiff professionalism. The false politeness of the ritual, automatic "have a nice day" at the conclusion of a business transaction is something you will never hear.

The robot-like professionalism which is drilled into so many clerks and bureaucrats in the United States, whether they be bank tellers, postal employees, or phone operators, simply is not practiced here.

In Israel you deal with human beings – pleasant or pressured, very nice or very rude. All contacts are on a strictly personal basis.

From the simplest to the most involved business transaction, Israelis treat customers in exactly the same way they themselves are treated: meaning, if you are rude, they are rude; if you are pressured, they are even more so.

But if on the other hand you make the effort to be nice, the Israeli clerk will respond (precisely because they are not used to such warmth) and light up like dawn over icy peaks. Great solace can be found if you do by chance happen to hear "have a nice day" from someone in Israel. You will know that it came from the heart.

CUSTOMS AND PRACTICES

No doubt the best news of this entire chapter is that one item which is not a part of Israeli business attire is the three-piece suit. Not even a two- or a one-piece either.

Unlike Joseph Conrad's colonial clerk in *Heart of Darkness*, whose "devotion to efficiency" included formal business dress despite the sweltering climate of the Belgian Congo, the Israeli weather has let the business community, lawyers and politicians off the hook.

But the weather is not the real reason. Beginning with David Ben-Gurion, informality has always been an integral part of the Israeli look. In fact, the open-collared short-sleeved shirt has become known over the years in Israel as the Ben-Gurion shirt.

The Israeli Businessman's Look

The Israeli businessman is, from top to bottom, informal but spruce, with respectable, often dressy shirts (always with solid colors), and without exception minus the gagging necktie. Add light summer pants and the picture is made complete by the most Israeli feature of all – sandals. Yes, even for the general manager of the most distinguished firm in the country, it's not only acceptable but customary to, as a Haitian friend of mine who hated sandals put it, "show your toes."

171

Typical Israeli business attire, minus the suit and tie.

The Israeli Businesswoman's Look

For the businesswoman, the dress code is far more similar to the standards of other countries. With the exception of the women of the kibbutz, Israeli women find themselves in much the same situation as other modern women around the world – still battling for their rights, trying to break through the barriers of primarily a man's world, and sometimes even dealing with sexist bosses.

Just as the American businesswoman takes these factors into account in deciding her attire, so too does the Israeli businesswoman. Female business dress is characterized by more informality, and perhaps by what could be called a lighter look, without the many layers one sees in colder climates. And not to forget, from the ground up, the businesswoman remains totally Israeli, with the customary, well-trodden sandals that manage to make all the country's citizens appear as if they just stepped out of the pages of the Bible.

Ways and Means

Don't be led astray by all this talk of informality. Israeli businessmen and women work extremely hard, and the fast pace of daily life, including the murderous 6-day week, often makes coping with the pressures a real battle. And in some cases, the unique Israeli approach adds to the burdens.

One example is that the telephone is used much less here than in other countries. Closing a business deal by phone is virtually unheard of in Israel; a personal, face-to-face meeting is almost always required. For the newcomer accustomed to the speed and convenience of dealing by phone, this can be one of the biggest culture shocks of doing business.

If the absence of the three-piece suit was the best news of the chapter, here comes, in my opinion, the worst. One phenomenon that does not exist in Israel is the three-martini lunch. (Not two or one either.)

When I explained to my friend, a top salesman in a telecom-munications firm who also happens to be a kibbutznik (yes, there are kibbutz businessmen; there was even a kibbutz advertising agency established recently), just what a three-martini lunch is, his response was classic: "How can they work after three martinis?"

When I attempted to outline for him the macho business tradi-tion of somehow being able to conduct efficient business while at the same time completely swackered (mercifully sparing him the historical/cultural background of Dashiell Hammett's *The Thin Man*, Winston Churchill's brandy, and Franklin D. Roosevelt's cocktail hour), the look he gave me hinted that I was totally out of my mind. He made me think twice about whether he was correct, especially as far as the three-martini lunch is concerned.

But considering the rat race here, perhaps it's a pity that three-martini lunches are not a custom. They could help break the tension of trying to do business while remaining sane at the same time.

TURNING THE TABLES

The correct translation of the familiar Hebrew phrase is really "turning over the table," but that is neither here nor there. What's important is that it refers to the most surprising – and most disagree-able – aspect of doing business in Israel.

The calmest of Israeli general managers (the very picture of level-headed business professionalism) will occasionally seem to deliberately lose his or her cool, start pounding on the desk while at the same time yelling, "What the hell is going on!" Just as he or she seems about to totally freak out (and turn over the table), the original quiet level tone is suddenly resumed as if nothing at all had happened. What is this? "This" is a typical Israeli performance – and that's just exactly what it is, a performance – which has become a routine and, worse, acceptable part of Israeli business conduct.

The custom of throwing a fit, whether because of the country's often exasperating bureaucracy or just due to the general pressures of everyday life, has become such an integral part of behavior here that Israelis believe, and perhaps rightly so, that nothing can possibly be accomplished without it.

Chutzpah

But there is no avoiding what could well be the real reason for such conduct. In a word (and it's Yiddish), it's what the Israelis call *chutzpah*. Insolence, audacity, brashness, rudeness, lack of politeness and decorum – define it as you will. It's this *chutzpah* which causes the tables to be turned, and often turns doing business into a nightmare.

One top Israeli executive explained it to me this way: In Israel, because the market is so small and the competition far less intense, the concept of service is much less developed than in other countries. So sometimes, in order to get what you want, you have no alternative but to yell and scream.

But what such a theory fails to take into account is the important part played in all this by the Israeli personality, which is about as far from the typical American model of executive self-control as you can get. It's this rough Israeli character, so well suited to the struggles and adversity of everyday life, that makes such abnormal conduct seem perfectly natural.

Perhaps the most curious part of this entire phenomenon is that after a short time in the country, foreigners inevitably find themselves adopting this behavior. Deliberately losing their temper with bureaucrats and clerks, exploding on cue with performances that would not disgrace the most veteran of Israelis, visitors find out that *chutzpah* is a contagious disease. And as far as doing business is concerned, it can unfortunately be very contagious indeed.

THE ISRAELI YUPPIE

Stroll around Tel Aviv and you cannot miss them. Lawyers, accountants, bank clerks, computer programmers; in short, the abbre-

An Israeli yuppie – quite different from his American counterpart – on the move.

viated "young urban professionals" with all their well-known acces-
sories – walkman, briefcase, newspaper or magazine under an arm,
eyeglasses in hand with which they gesture, each of them bearing
"the look" that has made the word "yuppie" so popular across the
developed world.

These ambitious, upwardly mobile young people have caused
many of the commercial musts of the yuppie lifestyle to bloom in
Tel Aviv: pizza joints with home delivery services (yuppies are
usually too busy to cook); expensive stores specializing in imported
running shoes (yuppies jog with the best); and lots and lots of
neighborhood pubs (despite the fact that Israeli yuppies remain true
to their heritage of not drinking). And worst of all, a few of them
have even begun to forsake the open-collared shirts and sandals for
three-piece suits and leather shoes!

Israel's emerging yuppie culture is but one example of a far
more widespread phenomenon: the Americanization of Israel. It's
not only the appearance of yuppies which makes many parts of Tel
Aviv seem so much like Downtown, USA; the shopping malls, the
specialty shops and restaurants (including yogurt and vegetarian
cafés) often make you feel as if you're in Los Angeles.

ARRIVING IN THE 21ST CENTURY

Business is even more susceptible to such influences than other
spheres of Israeli life. American business concepts, especially in the
marketing, advertising and public relations fields, are very prevalent. English has become the true second language of Israeli business, just as more and more English and American slang words have
found their way into the Hebrew vocabulary.

All the sophisticated playthings of American business – the
mobile telephones, beepers, fax machines and desktop computers –
have now materialized with all their annoying blips, bleeps, and
blats.

Not that Israelis make much use of them; at this stage they still remain more a symbol of business status than true tools of efficiency.

But little by little, the Israeli businessman and businesswoman are getting used to their new toys and integrating them into everyday practice.

As the 21st century approaches, one wonders whether anything at all will remain Israeli, at least as far as business is concerned. The following very Israeli response comes to mind: Of course there will – the bureaucracy and the *chutzpah*!

Chapter Ten

ISRAELI HOLIDAYS

"For transgression against God, the Day of Atonement atones; but for transgressions against a fellow man, the Day of Atonement does not atone so long as the sinner has not redressed the wrong done, and reconciliated the man he has sinned against."

—Rabbi Eleazar Ben Azariah.

IN LOVE WITH HOLIDAYS

Because of the quick pace of Israeli life, one soon notices that people live not only from day to day, but from holiday to holiday. With the New Year and Day of Atonement in the autumn, the Feast of Lights in the winter, Passover and Independence Day in the spring, and the Festival of Weeks with the coming of summer, life takes shape around these special landmark dates.

The holidays are central to the average Israeli – religious or secular – for the simple reason that with them come the long awaited, long yearned for vacation days. It's a time to rest, to take a breather, to gather strength to carry on with the daily battle that often characterizes Israeli life.

Jewish Holidays

The controversial description of Israel as a Jewish state (after all, non-Jews are Israeli citizens too) is especially relevant as far as the holidays are concerned. Christmas is for Jews a normal work day, as is the Moslem holy period of Ramadan. In these days, banks are open and life goes on as usual. And were it not for the news, one might not even notice that in much of the world these are major holidays. But during Jewish holidays, businesses come to a halt, stores close, streets are quiet, and Israeli citizens, whether they are Jewish, Moslem, Christian, Druze or Circassian, get a much appreciated day off.

But the holidays in Israel are much more than that. Not only do they preserve and sustain one of the oldest religions in the world, they also revitalize the ancient customs by adding many original and fresh elements. And what for centuries have traditionally been purely religious holidays have become something new: political and cultural celebrations which not only reflect the secular nature of Israeli life, but also commemorate Biblical history and the more recent events which shaped and molded the national personality. Indeed, one of the biggest surprises for newcomers is this revolu-

180

tionary side to what was previously known exclusively as religious holidays.

THE LUNAR CALENDAR

One important element of the holidays that has not changed is the ancient dating system which determines exactly when these special days will be celebrated every year.

Remaining true to centuries of Jewish tradition, the date of every holiday is based not on the Gregorian calendar that is known and familiar to all, but instead on the very different Hebrew calendar of the Bible – a time system that revolves around a lunar rather than a solar monthly cycle.

Now the subject of this book is Israel, not astronomy, so you are no doubt asking yourself the very Israeli question: "So what?" The answer provides yet another example of culture shock: Because of the Hebrew calendar system, every holiday in the country takes place on a different date every year. Confused? Just wait.

In very few countries in the world is buying a calendar as important as it is in Israel. There is simply no other way to know exactly when all of the holidays take place each year, unless you are accustomed to keeping time by the Bible. Even a holiday as secular as Independence Day – which marks the day on May 14, 1948 when Ben-Gurion proclaimed Israel's independence – is not celebrated on May 14 every year, but sometimes in the middle of April, some-times at the beginning of May, sometimes at the end of April, sometimes at the end of May. The date changes all the time. Why? The date May 14, 1948, according to the Hebrew calendar, was "the fifth day of the month of Iyar, 5708." Consequently, Independence Day is celebrated every year on the fifth day of the month of Iyar.

So what's the problem? The problem is that the difference between the two calendar systems (one lunar, the other solar) means that the fifth day of Iyar corresponds to the regular calender on a different day each year. Or to be exact, on each year except the 19th year, when due to the mathematics of the cycles, the two dates coincide. Having trouble following? Don't worry, the majority of Israelis feel the same way. In fact, most of the nation's citizens have very little understanding of the Hebrew calendar or how it works, and pay little attention to it.

But there is one thing Israelis do pay attention to: the absolute necessity of purchasing a calendar every year, which lets everyone know exactly when all of these precious holidays and vacation days are taking place.

Until I arrived in Israel, I never thought that I would miss something taken for granted: being able to count on the fact that a specific date like January 1 or December 25, year in and year out, (solar, lunar and interplanetary considerations aside) will always be a holiday!

The Count's Favourite Days

I cannot resist closing this section with an illuminating footnote, what should be of special interest to readers who happen to be vampires, werewolves or manic-depressives. One of the great advantages of the Hebrew calendar is that it's much easier to know precisely when there will be a full moon.

Unlike its rival system, where you must search through farmers' almanacs and astronomical charts to find out exactly when the moon will be lighting up the night sky in all its brilliance, in the Hebrew system all you have to do is wait for the middle of each month – the 15th to be exact.

Since every newspaper in Israel always prints the Hebrew date alongside the regular date, all you have to do is watch out for that magic number 15. Too bad Dracula was not born in Israel, or he would have found life much easier.

AUTUMN'S THE TIME

I have often thought about what it would be like to be some world-class bum, with no great love of the working life; who makes his way around the world and always seems to find a job in a country at precisely the moment when its most important holiday and vacation period is about to start.

Having deliberately planned the ultimate itinerary for someone who hates work, he travels from festival to festival, celebration to celebration, and from day off to day off. He spends Chinese New Year in the Orient, Lent in Rio de Janeiro, summer in Europe, Christmas and New Year's in the United States, and makes sure he arrives in Israel for fall.

Autumn in Israel offers a veritable bounty of much needed

Sounding the "shofar."

vacation time for the overworked Israeli. For nearly a month, the average week consists of both a holiday and the Sabbath day of rest – no small matter to a people used to working six-day weeks.

It all begins with the New Year or Rosh Hashana celebrations, which are followed 10 days later by Yom Kippur or the Day of Atonement. In another four days comes Sukkot or the Harvest Festival, and only another week goes by when there is yet another holiday: Simchat Torah, or the Rejoicing of the Law.

Autumn is a wonderful time to be in Israel. There's a real festive mood in the air; people who normally walk around frowning are smiling, and there is a noticeable drop in the nation's usually soaring blood pressure rate.

ROSH HASHANA

When the long anticipated New Year finally arrives, the festivities begin with a bang. One of the reasons why this holiday is so popular is neither religious nor secular, but simply because it's the only holiday all year long that has two consecutive "vacation" days.

Israel's citizens, especially immigrants who were once accustomed to working only five-day weeks, are virtually in shock to discover that they are facing the unbelievable prospect of two whole days off – a real honest-to-God weekend! With trips to the beach, picnics and barbecues on the shores of the Sea of Galilee, and hikes in the country's many national parks, the two-day holiday is like a massive nature festival, with lots and lots of eating in between.

The Period of Self-Examination

For the religious Jew, Rosh Hashana is of course much more than that. It's the beginning of the most important time of the year: the period of moral reckoning and self-examination of their conduct over the previous year. Spending many hours in the synagogue, the religious Jew attempts through worship and prayer to do the ethical accounting necessary to balance the scales of his or her life, and to get ready for God's judgment.

One of the high points of the holiday takes place when the ram's horn, or *shofar* as it is known in Hebrew, is trumpeted in order to "awaken the hearts of the faithful, and prepare them for repentance."

For Jews all over the world, the *shofar* is one of the most memorable symbols of the New Year. But for Israelis, it has also come to represent something more. In Israel's ancient history, the *shofar* was blown not only to herald the coming of the holidays, but to sound the alarm in times of war.

In modern Israel, such Biblical history is not merely a footnote to an ancient past, but also a living part of the people's mentality. This is best exemplified by the famous event involving one of the key incidents of Israel's Biblical history – the destruction of the Temple.

During the worst days of the 1973 Yom Kippur War, rumor has it that Defense Minister Moshe Dayan warned during a cabinet meeting of Israel's imminent defeat by uttering the now legendary sentence: "The Third Temple is falling." This is in reference to the two previous occasions when the Temple was destroyed by Babylonian and Roman conquerors, bringing to an end the two previous Jewish states.

It's no wonder that even for the most secular of Israelis, the sounding of the *shofar* is not only a symbol heralding the New Year, but of the national call to arms, a call that has sounded all too often in recent history.

YOM KIPPUR

While Rosh Hashana with its two-day vacation is the biggest holiday in Israel, Yom Kippur or the Day of Atonement is the single most important date on the calendar. In fact, Yom Kippur is the only holiday all year long in which the nation literally comes to a complete stop.

Radio and television stations go off the air, Ben Gurion Airport closes, and the streets are not merely void of traffic as on a normal holiday or the Sabbath, but totally deserted as if there is not a single car left in the entire country. In fact, one of the most delightful traditions of Yom Kippur is to walk down the middle of the biggest street in the city.

It cannot be denied that there is something very special about this holiday which defies words. Perhaps it can best be summed up by the almost eerie feeling of solemn peace and quiet that's in the air. Without cars and trucks, even the wind and the birds seem to be noisy – and it's a pleasant noise indeed.

Unlike major holidays in other countries, when despite the festivities some stores always manage to remain open (after all, money must be made), and the electronic media would never even think about shutting down (in the United States, there would be mass suicide), during Yom Kippur the entire nation – from airplane pilots to radio and television broadcasters – stop and take a much needed breath of fresh air.

The Holiest Day

For the religious Jew, Yom Kippur is the holiest day of the year, a climax to the moral introspection that began with Rosh Hashana and comes to an end, according to Biblical tradition, with God's judgment and forgiveness. The day is spent in the synagogue in heartfelt prayer and supplication, in repentance over the sins of the previous year.

It's also the time of the yearly fast. Between the two sunsets which open and close the holiday, observant Jews neither eat nor drink, and the token amount of suffering involved symbolizes the act of penitence so central to Judaism.

One curious aspect here is that even the most secular Israelis fast on Yom Kippur. The tradition of the holiday is apparently so deeply imbedded in the national character that it often goes beyond secular or religious barriers. Perhaps the feeling of repentance (along with the suggested hint of punishment) is such a powerful element in Yom Kippur that it has ingrained itself in the Israeli secular personality as well. But putting such attempts at national psychology aside, what has become a fundamental part of the holiday is one of the most pivotal and tragic events in Israel's history: the Yom Kippur War.

The 1973 Yom Kippur War

No Israeli will ever forget what happened in 1973, when the solemn peace of this most special day was shattered by Egyptian and Syrian armies launching a surprise attack.

October 6th – the shock of hearing the radio come on the air and secret army codes broadcast for the emergency call-up of all reserve units; the never to be forgotten scenes of men hurriedly leaving homes and synagogues and running to cars and buses after last farewells with their loved ones; the shock of seeing once deserted streets filled with rush-hour traffic.

But all these traumatic memories are but shadows of the biggest shock of all – the war itself; a war that was almost lost, and above all, a war in which the casualties – 3,500 Israeli soldiers killed – were, for a country as small as Israel, a terrible price that scarred the nation's soul.

The memories of that particular day have turned every Yom Kippur since into a kind of unofficial memorial day; a memorial to that war, to those who died in it, and to the nation which on that day somehow lost its innocence. From then on, Israelis have always associated Yom Kippur not only with a holiday, but with war.

SUKKOT

No sooner have Israelis recovered from the Yom Kippur fast that they are already preparing for the next holiday – Sukkot, or the Harvest Festival. The uniqueness of Sukkot is that it's the one celebration of the year which is clearly visible on the streets, in courtyards, on porches, balconies, and even on the roofs of houses. This is because the entire event revolves around the building of a *succah*, which in Hebrew means a temporary booth or shelter erected next to every religious home.

Turning all observant Jews into construction workers once a year, the *succah* is made of wooden boards, palm branches, thatch and leaves. Its exact specifications are set in the Old Testament. A symbol of the movable structure in which the ancient Israelites lived in during their exodus from Egypt, religious Jews must reside, or at least eat, in the *succah* for seven straight days.

Less symbolic, however, is the competition which invariably breaks out among these same people, the focus of which is the always quarrelsome question: Whose *succah* is more impressive? The following statement is usually heard quite loudly: "Yes, it's a beautiful *succah*, but it's not built according to Biblical rules!"

Sukkot is also the Harvest Festival, a time of traditional celebration and thanksgiving over the conclusion of the agricultural season. In Israel, it has naturally become one of the major holidays of the kibbutz. A kind of carnival with parades, children's games and parties, the kibbutz celebration has given its own unique, secular interpretation of Sukkot, as it has to most of the other holidays. So to the surprise of many, the secular kibbutznik often builds a *succah* too, not as a religious symbol of God's protection, but as a political metaphor for the *diaspora*, the "temporary home" of Jews around the world that has come to an end with the creation of the state of Israel.

SIMCHAT TORAH

A week after Sukkot, the last holiday of the autumn vacation extravaganza takes place – Simchat Torah, or the Rejoicing of the Law. A celebration of the Torah (the first five books of the Bible), Simchat Torah is a time of great joy for the observant Jew. This is the most purely religious of all the Israeli holidays because, surprisingly enough, it's the only religious celebration for which the Zionists have failed to come up with any secular interpretation whatsoever. But as far as the average Israeli is concerned, when a vacation from work is involved, he or she is glad to obey the Biblical commandment and take yet another day off!

HANUKKAH

Hanukkah, or the Feast of Lights, has in contrast become one of the most Israeli of all Jewish holidays. A celebration of national freedom and pride, it centers on the ancient Israelites' revolt against the Greek invaders, who turned the Temple into a shrine for Zeus and attempted to eradicate the Jewish faith.

The revolt and the victory which followed was led by an Israelite named Yehuda Maccabee. His name provides a classic example

The "menorah," the symbol of Israeli liberty.

of how Biblical history has become part of today's Israel. The annual national sports festival is called "the Maccabiah"; the best basketball team in the country is called Maccabee Tel Aviv; and most importantly (at least to me), the name of the number one selling beer in Israel is called – you guessed it – Maccabee.

The Menorah

One of the emblems of Israel, visible on Israeli coins and at the entrance to the nation's parliament, is the symbol of Hanukkah, the *menorah*.

The focus of Hanukkah is the lighting of the *menorah* candles – a candelabra made up of seven or eight separate branches – one during each of the eight nights of the holiday. The *menorah* has become not only a metaphor of Israeli liberty and freedom, but also one of the most important motifs in Israeli art. In nearly every home, there is usually some kind of a beautiful *menorah* displayed.

A Holiday Children Love

Hanukkah is one of the most enjoyable holidays of the year, not only because of the feasting, which according to Biblical tradition must take place during each of the eight nights, but because it's a holiday that children love. It is the children who get to light the Hanukkah candles each night (how kids love to play with fire), take part in the festivities that include games and parties, and eat the traditional Hanukkah jelly-filled doughnut. It is, after all, only fair that Hanukkah should be a children's holiday, coming as it does at approximately the same time as Christmas and Santa Claus.

A Holiday Adults Miss

But despite all the joys of Hanukkah, there is some bad news. Unfortunately for the hardworking Israeli, not a single one of the eight days is a public holiday or vacation day. Quite a disappointment, isn't it? Aggravating too, because if you don't get a day off for Hanukkah in Israel, where will you get it? The explanation won't help much either.

Religious holidays are vacation days in Israel only if they are mentioned in the Torah. If they are not, too bad. Thus Hanukkah is a piece of Biblical history which happened too late.

An interesting footnote is that Hanukkah also came too late for the Ethiopian Jews. When the war against the Greeks took place, these Ethiopians were still in exile in Africa. As a result, when they finally arrived in Israel, they had absolutely no knowledge whatsoever of Hanukkah, and had to learn from the beginning its history, meaning, and traditions.

PASSOVER

Revenge for the vacation-hungry Israeli comes at long last during spring, with the Passover holiday. Two days off (not consecutive but with a week between them) is the liberty granted for this day, which celebrates the liberation of the ancient Jewish people from Egyptian bondage. Few stories in the world are more famous, and to use an extremely American idiom, those who have not read the Book must surely have seen the movie. (Cecil B. de Mille and Charlton Heston be praised!)

What? No Bread?

But for the visitor, Passover is the one holiday you will never forget, because no other holiday will so directly touch your life. Why? Not because of its history, not because of the ceremonies that follow, but because during the entire week between the two vacation days there is virtually no bread in the land – not in stores, not in restaurants, and especially not in bakeries, which are closed during Passover.

During the week of Passover, Israeli residents and visitors alike must make do instead with the famous unleavened bread called *matzot*. *Matzot* for breakfast, *matzot* for lunch, and *matzot* for dinner. The symbol of the ancient Israelites' escape from Egypt, according to the Bible, the first *matzot* were eaten because there was not enough time to wait for the bread to be baked.

For those who have already heard about Passover and *matzot*, the surprise comes when finding out that it is not only bread that is forbidden, but all products containing yeast or any other leavening agent. It's beyond me to describe exactly what is included in this long list of forbidden foods, but suffice to say it includes quite a lot. You will find this out fast, because on Passover the familiar corner store where you do your shopping undergoes some very strange interior decoration. Entire shelves of food are covered with white sheets, making them off-limits for the holiday, and off your menu for that particular week.

For the religious, the Old Testament injunction forbidding these products also includes the command to rid your home of any trace of them. Thus one of the practical results of Passover is that a few days before the holiday, a massive wave of spring cleaning breaks out all over Israel. In an observant Jew's home, even the family couch is moved – not just for cleaning purposes, but in order to make sure that a lone noodle hasn't slipped behind the cushions!

So there is no escaping Passover in Israel (if you are interested in eating, that is). But for those really driven to desperation, it should be mentioned that there is always the possibility of traveling to Arab villages and buying pita bread in the local bakeries. But I would still recommend giving the breadless week a try. Over the years, I've found that this sudden change in the eating habits of an entire nation gives a unique personality to the holiday that is unforgettable. And *matzot* can be quite tasty.

The Passover Dinner

For the secular and religious Israeli alike, one of the biggest nights of the year is the Passover dinner ceremony. Called "the Seder" in Hebrew, this evening feast combines food and ritual to symbolically recreate the traditional tale of the ancient Israelites' exodus from

Egypt. Bitter herbs, for example, are eaten to symbolize the bitterness of Egyptian slavery. While eating other symbolic foods accompanied by wine, the Hagada, or traditional Exodus narrative, is read. What is interesting is that this traditional narrative has been translated into a countless number of versions, one quite different from the next. An experience not to be missed is the Passover ceremony on the non-religious kibbutzim, where sometimes the Biblical tale has been so secularized it's often hard to find any mention whatsoever of Moses. But here again, Passover is not just a Jewish religious ceremony but an Israeli holiday, adapted to accommodate all of the nation's citizens.

INDEPENDENCE DAY AND MEMORIAL DAYS

The most important thing to remember about both Independence Day and Memorial Day is that in Israel they are not the routine holidays taken for granted in most other countries. They are much, much more. This is best demonstrated by the fact that Israel's Independence Day always immediately follows the Memorial Day, making the inevitable link between the ceremony which celebrates the nation's pride, and the price for it which has been paid.

When Memorial Day officially begins during the evening, the opening ceremony at Jerusalem's Mount Herzl military cemetery is broadcast live on both radio and television. For the next 24 hours, the electronic media bombards the public with stories, films, documentaries, and interviews about famous Israeli battles and the soldiers who died in them. In a country which has been in a state of war since its creation, it is a time to honor the 17,500 soldiers who have fallen – some in the war of 1948, others in a firefight on the Lebanese border the previous day.

In every city, the most respected and honored citizens in the country – bereaved parents – make their yearly pilgrimage to the military cemeteries and local memorial sites. Although it is officially a work day in the country, during the morning hours the air raid sirens sound all over the nation, and an entire nation's people stop what they are doing and stand to observe a moment of silence in memory of the dead. (Since the Gulf War, the sounding of the sirens have invariably set off a panic among those unfamiliar with this annual Israeli ceremony, but nevertheless the tradition goes on.)

When Memorial Day comes to an end on the eve of Independence Day, the seemingly instant transition from solemnity to revelry is something striking to see. Israelis celebrate their independence with the all-out enthusiasm found only in the newest of countries; and this sudden transformation from sadness and bereavement to joy and celebration is almost cathartic in its intensity.

Independence Day is a nationwide carnival filled with parades, exhibitions, and musical events. Many cities in the country spend an entire year planning the festivities, which can include air shows, huge concerts, and the annual nightly fireworks.

Another tradition is that the Israeli army, navy, and air force always open up some of their bases, and the tours are a special treat, especially for the children. Yet even on this happiest of Israeli holidays, the price of independence is never forgotten.

One of the customs of Independence Day is for children to carry around a little plastic hammer and hit each other on the head with it, while at the same time saying the word "remember," thus reminding one another of the eternal link with Memorial Day. But as far as remembrance is concerned, I believe that the most extraordinary holiday is yet another Memorial Day – the Memorial Day to the Holocaust.

Holocaust Memorial Day

This day can be an unforgettable experience. The very first such day took place as early as December 2, 1942, several months after the first eyewitness accounts of Nazi concentration camps began to leak out of Europe. While the rest of the world refused to believe what was happening, on this day in 1942, the entire Jewish population of the British mandate of Palestine ceased work, spending the time fasting and praying for the Jews of Europe.

Holocaust Memorial Day has long since become a yearly tradition, and perhaps the most moving event in Israel. Although it is a regular work day, in the morning the air raid sirens again split the air, and the nation stands in a minute of silence – this time in remembrance of the six million who perished in the terrible event.

The entire day is spent with the country dedicating itself to retelling the terrible story. From the opening ceremony at the Yad VeShem Holocaust Memorial, which is broadcast on television and radio, to the myriad of documentary programs and interviews with survivors, the entire day focuses on educating those too young to know, and refreshing the memories of those who have forgotten. Indeed the official name of the event in Israel is not the Holocaust Memorial Day, but instead the Memorial to the Holocaust and the Heroism. This in reference to the instances, as in the Warsaw Ghetto Uprising of 1943, when Jews were not only victims but heroes.

One would think that year after year, bearing witness on Holocaust Memorial Day would become routine. The same ceremony at Yad VeShem every year, and the same survivors once again telling their terrible stories. But this is simply not so. Even those most familiar with the history find themselves touched and moved each year. I personally thought I had heard or read all the stories – from mothers forced to choose between saving a son or a daughter, to all the grisly macabre tales of the concentration camps. But a memorable one was an interview with a survivor who was a slave laborer sent to dig up and destroy the mass graves of Jews massacred by the Nazis.

This survivor told of how one of his fellow Jews, one of the toughest men among them, placed the dead body of a pregnant woman on the blazing outdoor pyre which burned up the corpses. The belly of the woman swelled with the heat and when it burst, the body of her dead baby flew out.

The survivor told how this man tenderly picked up the dead baby, took it in his arms, and said in a choked voice of sadness and despair: "Good that you'll never know what this world is, my child … good that you'll never know." I shall remember that interview for as long as I live; it was but one of many such testimonials of those bearing witness.

SHAVUOT

The yearly procession of major Israeli holidays, with both their sadness and joy, comes to an end with Shavuot, the Festival of Weeks. Shavuot, which means weeks in Hebrew, refers to the seven weeks it took the ancient Israelites to reach Mount Sinai after their escape from Egypt. There, Moses received the Ten Commandments and the Torah. For the religious Jew, Shavuot is therefore a commemoration of the giving of the Torah, and for centuries of Jewish life in the *diaspora*, this was the sole meaning of the holiday.

But in Israel, another important tradition has developed. Here, Shavuot has also become a celebration of the land and of agriculture, and consequently has turned into *the* kibbutz holiday. A delightful carnival-like event which includes parades, along with the ceremonial presentation of all the kibbutz crops ("the fruits of the land"), Israelis from all over the country flock to the kibbutzim on Shavuot.

On this the last vacation day before the hot Israeli summer, it is the customary time to take a deep breath and get ready to bear down for the long haul until September, when the yearly holidays again begin anew.

A FEW MINOR HOLIDAYS
Purim

Taking place in the early spring, this is even more of a holiday for children than Hanukkah. What Halloween is to the United States, Purim is to Israel. The streets are filled with kids in costume (not

Children all dressed up to celebrate Purim, Israel's version of Halloween.

Biblical characters, but rather Batman, Dracula, and the ever-present Ninja). The holiday commemorates the story of the ancient Persian Jews, who were sentenced to be exterminated by their Persian rulers led by a man called Haman. But they were able to turn the tables on him instead; Haman was executed, and the Jews were allowed to prosper.

An interesting footnote to this holiday is this is the only time of the year when the ultraorthodox Jews are permitted to get drunk!

Tisha B'av

The ninth day of the Hebrew month of Av, which falls in the summertime, this is the saddest day of the year for the religious Jew. A commemoration of destruction that twice came on the Temple, it is a time of mourning for all the misfortunes that have befallen the Jewish people during their long history.

On Tisha B'av, there are literally thousands of people at the Western Wall. So for the visitor, it is recommended to take a look. It's quite a sight.

May Day

No, this isn't yet another Jewish holiday, but the very same May Day of Karl Marx and the Soviet Union. Israel, with its socialist economic system and ideological Russian roots, still celebrates this holiday, and until recently it was even an official vacation day.

It still is on the calendar of the nation's kibbutzim, many of which fly the red flag on May Day. But with the collapse of communism all over the world, one can only wonder how long this will last.

— *Chapter Eleven* —

DAILY LIFE

"The father supplies the white substance of which the child's bones, sinews, nails, brain and the white of the eyes are formed. The mother supplies the red substance of which are formed the skin, flesh, hair, blood, and the dark of the eyes. God supplies the spirit, the breath, beauty of features, eyesight, hearing, and the ability to speak and to walk, understanding and discernment."

—H. Schneid (ed.), *Family*.

THE OLD AND THE NEW

Daily life in Israel is, like the country itself, a combination of the old and the new. With all the modern supermarkets, computerized checkout counters, and huge shopping malls, you are also likely to find on the street where you live an old guy selling fresh fruit off his horse-drawn cart. Riding up and down the street past your apartment or house each morning, he goes about proclaiming like a town seer "Apples! Bananas! Watermelons!" in a call which sounds like it hasn't changed since Biblical times.

With the Americanization of the world consumer market, where hamburger chains, Coca-Cola, and seemingly identical shopping centers have turned the entire globe into "USA Inescapable," daily life in Israel still manages to maintain its cultural uniqueness. And the best news of all is that, at the time of writing, Israel remains one of the few developed countries on the planet where McDonald's, Burger King and Kentucky Fried Chicken have yet to arrive.

SHOPPING

Shopping in Israel can be great fun. This no doubt comes as good news to those bored by the routine drudgery of the weekly trip to the grocery store. Of course the big supermarket chain, with its bright lights and canned music, does exist in Israel (here it is called the Super-Sol), but there are some interesting differences.

One of the most enjoyable parts of culture shock in Israel is strolling up and down the aisles of these supermarkets, figuring out how the different Israeli products compare with what you are accustomed to back home. For example, dishwashing liquid is actually a sort of thick yellow glop which comes in a blue plastic bucket, and milk comes not in bottles or cartons but clear amorphous plastic sacks, which more than anything else so obviously resemble blood or plasma bags that you will be tempted to ask for a milk transfusion.

Israeli food manufacturers have tried to keep up with the times

The Israeli nutcracker suite: nuts galore in an Israeli market.

by marketing lots of fast foods, vegetarian dishes, fancy frozen meals, and even a homegrown Israeli soy sauce (which is definitely not recommended). But it soon becomes clear that for all their efforts, there is still a very marked difference between Israeli groceries and what you are used to buying back home. Here, for instance, you will still find only three or four different kinds of salad dressing, instead of the usual 50 or 60 which take up an entire aisle in American supermarkets.

The Imports Have Arrived

However, even this has been changing in recent years. A free trade agreement with the United States, along with expanded trade with Europe and the Far East, have brought a myriad of mouth-watering items to Israel's supermarket shelves. Israeli consumers have even been graced lately with Italian pasta; for spaghetti lovers, you can't do better than that. There is soy sauce from Taiwan, "Hero" jam from Switzerland, and even some of those 60 varieties of American salad dressing.

In Israel, imports have become "in," and many of the country's once ordinary butcher shops have now turned into "specialty stores," stocking their shelves with all sorts of luxury goods from around the world. But consider yourself warned: imports are very expensive in Israel. Yet even if you can afford to spend all your money on imported foods, it would be a shame to miss out on some of the local Israeli specialities, and not only because they are so cheap.

Chicken, fish and lamb are all relatively inexpensive, but the real bargains are the agricultural products: fresh fruits, vegetables, and even nuts (almond, walnut, pecan, cashew, filbert, peanut, pistachio, sunflower seed – all fresh, tasty and so cheap that Israelis have turned nutcracking into a national pastime).

For lovers of fresh fruit, whether because of health benefits or merely good taste, Israel could be the best place in the world. There is everything from citrus (in more varieties than you can imagine, some of which have been genetically "invented" by Israel's agricultural experts) to apples, bananas, avocados, mangos, loquats, you name it. Thanks to the miracle of Israel's agricultural technology (the world leader in the field), they are all homegrown, fresh and, most importantly, surprisingly cheap. I especially get a kick out of the Israeli bananas. How in God's name can you grow bananas in the desert? But the Israelis do it, and in addition to enjoying their delicious taste, you can also get satisfaction out of the fact that you are not exploiting some poor South American peasant by buying them. All of this treasure-house of produce can easily be purchased at the supermarket, but a much cheaper and far more enjoyable place to go is the famous Israeli *shuk*.

Shuk

Shuk is the Arabic word for open-air market, and the word, like the phenomenon, has become an integral part of Israeli culture. Every town in the country has its own *shuk*, where laid out on tables is a rich bonanza of fresh fruits and vegetables at extremely low prices.

Shopping in the Israeli *shuk* is an experience, not only because of the amazing array of colorful fresh fruits and vegetables. The sellers themselves seem to have stepped out of another century, all of them shouting out their prices and bargaining with each customer in a cacophony of noise which is typically Middle Eastern.

I even know of a linguistics professor who has made a study of the accents of the *shuk*, and from the way one hears "bananas" trumpeted out each time in a different lilt and inflection, there are plenty of them.

These days, another striking aspect of the *shuk* is that it's always filled with Russian immigrants. Not just looking for bargains, their eyes still seem to fill with wonder at the incredible display of Israeli produce, no doubt remembering how at the comparable Soviet *shuk* they had to stand in line for hours to buy their monthly allotment of potatoes.

The Israeli "shuk" doesn't just feature fruits and vegetables. The "shuk" pictured here sells everything from clothes and shoes to toiletries and other goods.

Mekolet

Another unique aspect of the Israeli shopping experience is what is known in Hebrew as the *mekolet*. A small neighborhood grocery, this is Israel's answer to the 7-Elevens, mini-markets and convenient stores. There is not a neighborhood in Israel that does not have one or even several *mekolet*, and not a home or apartment that is not within walking distance of one of these family-owned shops.

Although quite small (usually occupying part of the ground floor of an apartment building), these shops not only have many of the essentials which you can suddenly run out of – like eggs, milk or sugar – but often carry a surprising amount of other items as well. With the hectic pace of Israeli life, this can be a big help, because when you are too tired or lazy to make the trip to the center of town for your weekly purchases, you can easily take a stroll into the neighborhood store. Indeed many people pass up the supermarket altogether, and do all their shopping here.

Surrounded by an intensely personal shopping atmosphere, it is always warm and friendly in the *mekolet*, which also functions as a kind of neighborhood community center. And the most Israeli aspect is that nobody ever seems to pay! The average customer walks in, says hello to Yossi, Elana, or whoever else is working, and after picking out his or her purchases, the products are priced, added up and written on a small index card kept behind the counter (computers have not yet reached the *mekolet*). In principle, everybody is supposed to pay at the end of the month, but whether they actually do or not is another question.

MONEY MATTERS
Home Hunting

It is with the dollar-wise practicalities of life that the daily Israeli rat race shifts into high gear. The first obstacle is usually renting a house or apartment. Russian immigration has turned what used to be a rather routine task into a virtual mission impossible. Massive

A "mekolet" in Tel Aviv.

housing shortages, giant rent increases and, worst of all, wherever you look, an explosion in the number of not entirely legitimate real estate agents.

Sadly, finding a house or apartment in Israel has turned into a war, with the real estate market a battlefield complete with land mines. Apartments in the big cities of Tel Aviv, Haifa, and Jerusalem were never cheap to begin with, but with the demand of thousands of Russian Jews (along with the inexcusable lack of government regulation), prices have skyrocketed. You can easily pay $500 a month for a two-room apartment these days; not terribly expensive rent compared with New York, Paris or Tokyo, but as far as Israel is concerned, outrageously high.

Seeking Help Through Real Estate Agents

In today's market, it's almost impossible to find a house or apartment without a real estate agent. A few years ago, it was much easier; in order to locate something reasonable, it was enough to merely take a glance through the classified ads of *The Jerusalem Post*. These days, nothing is reasonable, and unless you have got lots of time to hunt, only the "experts" can help you find what you're looking for.

In Israel, it's standard for real estate agents to take your first month's rent. That's legitimate. The problem is that so many illegitimate agents have recently sprung up. (In Hebrew, they are called "mediators," though *karish* – meaning shark – would be a much more appropriate translation.) Trustworthy, accredited real estate agents who have been around long before the Russians arrived are few and far between, but one agency I can recommend (not only because of its name) is the Anglo-Saxon. They have offices nationwide, in nearly every city.

But not to worry because, in spite of it, all foreign residents in Israel usually have no problems finding an apartment. This is due to the fact that Israeli landlords prefer to deal with those paying in

American dollars rather than in the ever fluctuating Israeli currency, the *shekel*.

But after you have found a house or apartment, coming to an agreement with your landlord can be difficult. Some demand leases and contracts, a security deposit, or even a year's rent in advance; while others prefer to keep the whole transaction informal and personal, and are much more flexible about payment. One of the advantages of using accredited real estate agents is that they can help you get through these negotiations successfully.

Once you are settled in, a few words about the typical Israeli landlord. He or she is usually incredibly stingy, so don't expect to get the walls painted and fixtures repaired at no cost. On the other hand, if you are lucky, you could end up with a Jewish mother-type who will take good care of you.

In addition to the monthly rent, tenants are also expected to pay the city taxes on the house or apartment, known in Hebrew as the infamous *arnona* or municipal tax. Those in apartments will also have to shell out a small monthly sum for the upkeep of the building, which is called, for reasons only Israelis are capable of understanding, "the house committee" payment.

Banking Basics

Israelis are among the biggest bankers in the world. Whether due to the instability of the Israeli currency, the multitude of credit and savings plans, or even the fact that they are open for business six days a week, the banks always seem to be teeming with customers.

All the up-to-date innovations of modern banking are now available: the money machines, from which you can withdraw cash at any time of the day or night (called "Caspo-mats"); banking by mail, including 24-hour deposits; telephone banking; even banking via your home computer.

Taking advantage of all these services is even more important in Israel than in other countries because the more you can avoid

209

Standing in line – an unavoidable part of Israeli life.

actually stepping into the bank itself, the better. Whole mornings can disappear while waiting your turn in the long lines of the crowded Israeli banks.

Israelis are big bankers for another reason. Very few people keep their money in only one account. Immigrants and foreign visitors are allowed to hold dollar accounts, while most Israelis keep their savings (if they have any) in one of the myriad of high interest bank plans which are linked to the dollar. Through their ordinary *shekel* accounts, which usually don't bear interest, people pay out their checks, daily bills, and credit card payments.

What has become an incredible phenomenon here is the infamous Israeli "minus." Having a balance of zero *shekel* in your bank account is actually an advantage in Israel, because it is routine practice for Israelis to go thousands in the red each month. This is allowed by the banks, which rake in huge profits from the penalties.

If the average Israeli is in good financial shape, the gaping hole of his or her deficit will be automatically brought back to zero every 30 days, when monthly salaries are automatically transferred into *shekel* accounts.

The nation's financial practices, more than any other aspect of life, are the source for the familiar axiom that Israelis live from month to month. And matters are only made worse by another very popular item: the long-term payment.

Buying hundreds or even thousands of dollars worth of products or services, and spending two or three years paying them off, is common practice for many Israelis. If all this sounds like the United States in the Roaring '20s (and just as inevitably a prescription for economic disaster), you will get no argument from me.

THE ISRAELI WELFARE STATE

Israeli society is characterized by a very large middle class. Unlike the United States – a nation of winners and losers, where a powerful upper class is paralleled by an equally large, if not larger, lower

211

class – Israel is dominated by a vast majority in the middle, with a lucky few rich at the top, and a scattering of less fortunate at the bottom.

Whether because of its socialist heritage, or merely the bad luck of not being graced with oil like other countries in the Middle East, the lion's share of Israelis are salaried workers who live in apartments and somehow manage to make ends meet. The typical Israeli apartment block, usually a five- or six-floored stone or concrete structure, is so prevalent that it has given an identical, East European look to virtually all of Israel's cities and towns, from Kiryat Shemona in the north to Beersheba in the south.

An integral part of this middle-class reality is that Israel is a welfare state in the classic social-democratic mold. Free public education, in which parents have the choice of sending their children to either a religious or secular state school, along with government subsidized universities and health care, have all made Israeli society extremely egalitarian.

But this has had its price, and not only in high taxes. The bureaucracy which plagues the business sector is nothing compared to the number of institutions which surround the private citizen, from the government ministries which totally support the immigrant in his or her first year in the country, to those which pay ordinary citizens everything from unemployment benefits, veteran and child care payments, and even financial compensation for time spent in the military reserves.

The Public Health Establishment

One of the biggest institutions in the nation is the huge public health establishment, which provides the entire population with low-cost medical care. Contrary to many of the horror stories you hear about socialized medicine, I personally have received very good care over the years from the biggest of the public health organizations, the Histadrut "Kupat Holim," or Sick Fund.

From the small neighborhood clinic with its familiar family doctor, and the medical center in the middle of town with its many specialists, to the big hospitals for emergency treatment, my experience has by and large been positive. If you can manage to ignore the inevitable by-products of socialized medicine – the multitude of forms, the long waits, and the standing in line – then you will discover, often with surprise, that what should be the bottom line – good medical care – is indeed available in Israel.

In recent years, however, something new has appeared on the traditionally socialist Israeli scene: privatization. In the big cities, private doctors, private medical clinics, and even private hospitals are beginning to establish themselves, with the goal of serving those with enough money to bypass the large medical bureaucracy.

Although the trend is still only in its infant stages, the powerful Israeli health care unions have already begun to let out a howl of protest over these "medical services for the rich." It seems unlikely that Israel will ultimately develop into a country like the United States, where the top medical services are only available to those who can afford them. But in any case, it's important for foreigners or visitors to keep in mind that even though they can join the big public health organizations at relatively low cost, private medical care has become an option.

In fact the potential resident, especially if he or she is wealthy, should know that like virtually every other country in the world, all the amenities of the upper class are available. From private schools in English or French (or a number of other languages) to maids, cooks, and even chauffeurs – they can all be found, at a cost.

The small elite community of rich Israelis is congregated in a few select neighborhoods of Tel Aviv, Haifa, and Jerusalem, as well as in seaside resort towns like Caesaria (where Israel's one and only golf course is located). And as irrelevant as it is to the vast majority of Israelis, I have even read that the newest fad among the Israeli rich is hiring an imported maid from the Philippines.

DRIVING IN ISRAEL

This topic could be the subject of an entire chapter (if not a separate book) because regardless of the possibility of war or terrorist attack, there is no doubt what the single most dangerous part of living in Israel is: driving.

Israelis are among the worst drivers in the world. An average of 450 traffic fatalities a year – two and a half times the rate of northern Europe – is but one of the statistics which characterizes this, the most dangerous of Israel's national quirks. Speeding, overtaking on curves, passing on hills, not signalling – it's the Wild West as far as driving is concerned. And if you think cars are going to stop when you cross a street, then I can recommend some less painful ways to commit suicide.

Israel is one of the few countries in the world where a yellow light is not a warning to get ready to stop but rather a signal to get ready to go, and "going" in Israel often means putting your foot down on the gas and, if you are religious, saying a prayer or two. Even those who decide to forego driving (though it's easy enough to exchange your foreign driver's license for an Israeli license) find that there is no way to avoid this national disease.

Taking a bus trip in Israel, say from Jerusalem to Tiberius in the north or Eilat in the south, can be a beautiful ride. The scenery along the Jordanian border is truly spectacular, and the Mercedes buses are very comfortable. But unfortunately it can also be an unforgettable journey for another reason: the average Israeli bus driver usually takes the winding, mountainous route so fast that the bus seems to be literally taking the turns on two wheels. Consequently, you might just learn the hard way that Israeli buses, unlike jets, don't carry air sickness bags.

Psyching Israeli Drivers

What are the reasons for such suicidal behavior? There are several, but before dealing with them, it's important to note that even if you

Your typical Israeli bus, with all the necessary comforts that buses around the world offer ... except for the reckless driver.

are the safest driver in the world, there are other factors which contribute to the high rate of danger.

To put it simply, the roads in this country are terrible. Narrow highways, some of them in atrocious condition, make for hazardous driving. Worst of all, on Israeli highways there is no margin for error; that essential half lane on the side of the road which gives you the vital space to recover in the event of an accident, blowout, or even a miscalculation, simply does not exist. In Israel, any driving mistake you make could well be your last.

Also, unlike most developed countries, Israel has no highway patrol or traffic police to enforce its laws. The nation's hard-pressed police force has little time for traffic offenses when every day is spent dealing with preventing terrorism and constant demonstrations, not to mention crime. Manpower shortages and budgetary restraints have continued to prevent the formation of a highway patrol, despite the public outcry which goes up with each horrendous accident, and with the publication of the yearly traffic fatality statistics.

Yet money problems don't just affect the police. Another big contributor to the high accident rate is that the average Israeli, just barely making ends meet, does not have much to spend on cars, or especially on upkeep and repair. It's incredible – and if you are driving, terrifying – to see the number of wrecks on Israeli roads. And considering their condition, it's a wonder that these cars actually move from place to place, much less stop when they are supposed to.

But there is no doubt that at the heart of the problem is the unique Israeli personality. Jerusalem's famous mayor, Teddy Kolleck, was once asked why he thought Israelis were such terrible drivers.

"When you have to fight a war once every 10 years," he replied, "safe driving becomes the farthest thing from your mind."

I have not given this interpretation much thought until recently, when yet another tragic car accident made headline news in Israel. The only son of Ezer Weizman, one of the country's most respected leaders, was killed while speeding on the Tel Aviv-Haifa highway.

During the early 1970s, while serving as a front line commander in the paratroops, this young man had been shot in the head by an Egyptian sniper. Many believe that the trauma of his critical wounding was what transformed his father from a hawkish warrior and air force general – the architect of Israel's victory in the Six Day War – to the dovish politician who led the way to peace with Egypt. Of Weizman's son, it was said that his terrible wound, along with his long struggle to recover, made death for him a very familiar companion. Like so many other Israelis, he finally found it on one of the nation's highways.

THE ESSENTIALS OF DAILY LIFE
Emergency Services
100 is the phone number for police in the big cities; 101 for ambulances and medical help; and 102 for the fire department. Israel, as mentioned, is well served by hospitals, from several in each of the major cities (the largest are Haddassah in Jerusalem, Tel HaShomer in the Tel Aviv area, and Rambam in Haifa) to the regional medical centers which provide services to everyone in northern or southern Israel.

Telephone and Postal Services
The telephone service in Israel is rated from fair to poor. Compared to other modern developed countries it is, to say the least, disappointing. Lots of disconnections, wrong numbers, and faulty lines are yet another aspect of the frustrating part of Israeli life. But do not despair, things are getting better. For example, it's possible now to dial direct to most countries, and collect calls can be made by dialing 188.

The postal service, on the other hand, is not bad, and in many

217

ways is just as efficient (or inefficient) as that in the United States. Express mail services are available domestically and internationally, as is the infamous facsimile (fax) service.

Water

It is safe to drink water direct from the tap anywhere in the country. (You can easily tell which tourists have just arrived from Egypt, because they are the ones who still insist on buying their drinking water.)

An interesting fact about Israel's water: it comes from one and only one source – the Sea of Galilee. This, the world's most famous lake, provides all of the country's drinking and irrigation water. Indeed, Israel's problems with water are but one element in the larger crisis which grips the entire Middle East; in fact, experts guess that the next war in the region will not be over oil, the Territories, Palestinian rights or Zionism, but over water.

Currency

The exchange rate for the Israeli *shekel* is, on the average and at the time of writing in 1991, two and a half *shekel* to the US dollar. But beware – inflation has been known to frequently rage in Israel, making devaluations and even changes in the denominations of the currency a common occurrence. At present, there are 5, 10, 50 and 100 *shekel* bills.

Weather

Mediterranean climate; summers are hot and winters warm, with cool evenings. From April to October, the temperature averages from 23 C to 30 C. From November to March, it's 15 C to 20 C. From November to March, there may be periods of heavy rain. Keep in mind that in Jerusalem, summers are a bit cooler (and more comfortable) than in Tel Aviv, while the winters are warmer on the coast, and cooler in the capital.

Clothes

Light clothing may be worn all year round, although a sweater is required during the winter, especially in the evenings.

Tipping

A 10 percent service charge is usually included in hotel and restaurant bills. If not, then a 10 to 15 percent tip is enough.

Banks

Banking hours are from 8:30 a.m. to 12:30 p.m. and from 4 p.m. to 5 p.m. Banks are closed on Monday, Wednesday and Friday afternoon, and of course on Saturday and holidays.

Government and Business Offices

Working hours are from 7:30 a.m. to 2:30 p.m. (June to October) and from 7:30 a.m. to 1 p.m. and 1:45 p.m. to 4 p.m. (November to May). Offices are closed on Friday afternoon and Saturday.

Transportation

Metered taxis are expensive and it's not necessary to tip taxi drivers. Airconditioned buses, under the Israel bus cooperative known as Egged, cover the country with comfortable, cheap and frequent services. The buses do not run Friday evenings and Saturdays, or during the holidays.

Airport

Ben Gurion International is about 19 kilometers from Tel Aviv. Taxi rates from Ben Gurion to all major cities are listed on signs at the airport.

Eating

There are many restaurants in Jerusalem, Tel Aviv, Haifa and Eilat serving international cuisines. Some are kosher, some are not.

219

Tourist Information

See the Israel Government Tourist Information Office in two locations:

• The Jerusalem office at 24 King Street, Tel: (02) 241581
• The Tel Aviv office at 7 Mendele Street, Tel: (03) 223266

— *Chapter Twelve* —

YOU'RE AN ISRAELI

walking the Israeli Walk...

"Ruth answered, 'Do not urge me to go back and desert you. Where you go, I shall go, and where you stay, I shall stay. Your people will be my people, and your God my God.' "

—Ruth 1:16-18

THE SABRA'S WAY

Like deep-sea divers who get the bends if they spend too much time underwater, after a short time in Israel, the way of life, the mentality, and above all the Israelis themselves will begin to have an effect on you.

It is no accident that native-born Israelis are known as *sabras* – named after the cactus fruit which is tough and thorny on the outside but surprisingly sweet on the inside. Don't expect to grow thorns after a few months in the country, it's not quite as bad as all that. But most do find that the classic Israeli toughness, whether in talk, conduct, or mannerisms, is bound to rub off.

TALKING THE TALK

You don't have to know Hebrew to be familiar with what George Orwell might have called "Israel-speak." A polyglot combination of words and phrases from several different languages and cultures, they invariably have a multitude of meanings. And most of them, no doubt due to the hectic pace of Israeli life, have to do with impatience and aggravation.

Yallah

One such example is the Arabic word "yallah." An essential part of the Israeli vocabulary, depending on the situation and the mood of the speaker, it can mean anything from "Let's go" and "Please hurry" to "Get a move on, for Pete's sake!" But it can also be an expression of amazement. Instead of the American "Wow," or the even stronger "Holy —," Israelis will shake their heads and let loose a long "yaa-aallahh." At the same time, it can signify the Israeli seal of approval on a difficult business transaction, as if to say, "Well, we've finally agreed, now let's get on with the task – yallah."

My best friend always concludes his telephone conversations with a softly spoken "ya-llah," as if to say, "Well, we've covered everything in this particular talk, so until we meet again, be well."

Yet five minutes later, it will be shouted in heavy traffic as a swear word to prompt the old lady driver holding up things to get the lead out of her —!

Nu

The most important Yiddish contribution to Israel-speak is the word "nu." Roughly translated as "so," it has about 200 other meanings, depending on the mood of the speaker. A typical Israeli greeting is not "How are you" but rather "Nu, how are you," as if to say, "So – it's obvious with the insane pace of Israeli life that you couldn't possibly be OK, but in any event I'm asking." The corresponding response is usually, "Nu, how should I be?" It's as if this one word expresses all the suffering which, according to the Yiddish-Jewish mentality, is already taken for granted.

Yet "nu" can also be the tough Israeli one-word response to that suffering. Meaning everything from "Did you expect anything different?" and "Life is no picnic" to "So what?" it is the classic Israeli expression of both indifference and acceptance.

Israel's most popular political satirist, Shlomo Nizan, begins every one of his monologues with the one-word question "Nu?" – and the audience is already laughing in anticipation of his merciless attacks on the country's insufferable politicians and bureaucrats.

And not to be forgotten, "nu" is also a word which is synonymous with great impatience and aggravation. ("Nu – did you expect anything different?") In that long line at the bank which does not seem to move, you will no doubt hear someone sigh and let out an irritated "nnnuuuu." Or once again in that same traffic jam behind that same poor old lady, the Israeli driver will curse her by sticking his head out of the window and shouting an exasperated: "Nnnuuu!!!"

Zey Ma Yesh

But there is no way to avoid the Hebrew language when describing two of the most popular Israeli sayings, sentences which best epito-

223

mize what it is to be an Israeli.

The first is "Zey ma yesh" (That's what there is). Although harried and often under considerable pressure, Israelis are definitely not complainers, and they have a long tradition of "making do with what there is" (which often hasn't been much).

Routinely facing situations which other people would find intolerable, Israelis, especially in difficult times, are known for their capacity for keeping their noses to the grindstone, their spirits high, and for substituting all the whining and complaining with the simple utterance "that's what there is." Indeed, this is one of the most oft-repeated sentences, because it automatically comes in place of the lamentable "I can't believe this," the angry "How can this be," or even the outraged "What a screwed-up country this is!" Israelis will shrug, shake their heads and merely say, "Zey ma yesh."

In the Israeli Army, this traditional expression has an additional phrase tacked on to it: "That's what there is – and with it we will win."

Ye-Heye Besedr

The other classic Hebrew sentence is "Ye-heye besedr" (All will be well). This simple expression of optimism and hope has, more than any other phrase, become the motto of the Israeli people. From the worst moments of the Iraqi missile attacks during the Gulf War to the normal day-to-day rat race, this is the sentence one hears most from Israelis in the worst possible situations; not the hopeless "What will we do?" or "Where will it all end?" or the even more poignant "God help us," but instead the active pledge that "all will be well." In its brevity and simplicity, this sentence has come to symbolize the single most impressive characteristic of the Israelis: their ability to remain, in spite of it all, an essentially optimistic, hopeful and upbeat people.

Perhaps the best illustration of this can be found in the last words of one of Israel's most legendary heroes, Yonotan Netanyahu, who commanded and was killed in the famous 1976 Entebbe rescue operation. After his death, Netanyahu's personal correspondence was published in Hebrew in a book called *Yoni's Letters*. (The English translation was more fittingly entitled *Self-Portrait of a Hero*.)

In a truly moving letter written only five days before his death, Netanyahu, up to that time one of the most successful and highly decorated officers in the Israeli Army, showed his first signs of pessimism, wondering where it would all end in this crazy world of non-stop battles in a never-ending war. Yet even here, in this his first expression of doubt and despair, he concludes with the words "Ye-heye besedr" – all will be well. Little could he know then that these, the last words of a man who would come to represent more than any other the exemplary model of the Israeli hero, would become a kind of blessing for Israel and its people.

WALKING THE WALK

One of the essential prerequisites of "walking the Israeli walk" is the very distinctive Israeli look. From top to bottom, it includes a short hairstyle (for both men and women), sunglasses (usually the Israel air force-type), a cigarette (unfortunately, whether due to the army or other pressures, an astonishingly high percentage of Israelis smoke), and of course the unforgettable Israeli sandals. For both sexes, it is a macho look, and not only just a look – acting like an Israeli often translates into a kind of latent machismo.

Israeli Machismo

Indeed, Israel must be one of the most "macho" countries on Earth. In business and social situations, typical Israeli behavior is often quite cold, and Israelis are not big on touching and other intimate forms of social contact.

This roughness can also include a lack of table manners. While dining, many Israelis simply point to what they want or merely say

Hold your horses – in Israel-speak, that is. This is the polite way of saying "wait a minute," without uttering a word, but with hand raised and fingers pursed together.

"pass the bread" without the automatic "please." And all this applies as much, if not more, to the battle of the sexes: the image of the thorny *sabra* is especially relevant to the single Israeli girl.

Except for the religious, Israeli girls are as remiss about obeying the Ten Commandments as their fellow females around the world, but this does not stop them from putting up the icy Israeli front. Those looking to chat up the object of their desires by using well-practiced techniques proven on European or American girls could well find themselves getting pricked by the Israeli *sabra*.

I personally have found that many Israeli girls don't quite know how to deal with courtesy and gentlemanly behavior. An act as bizarre as holding the door open for your date can be greeted with astonishment, followed by a strange look. This reaction is not, as it might be in other countries, a result of feminism, but rather pure shock at not being treated in the usual chilly Israeli manner. In fact, most Israeli men remain extremely chauvinistic. This even extends to the language. In Hebrew, "woman" and "wife" can mean exactly the same thing – they are one in the same word.

Israeli Mannerisms

With few exceptions, the average Israeli likes to be thought of as the strong, silent type, a man or woman of action, not words. This is conveyed for the most part in not expressing much; that is, in not saying much, being brief, and even being what might be described in other countries as curt.

A good case in point involves Israeli mannerisms. In situations which call for politely saying "wait a minute" or "please hold on," Israelis are known to refrain from uttering a word, and will instead inexplicably raise their hand and purse their fingers together. Is this some kind of Israeli obscenity? After all, the middle finger is involved. No, this gesture means in Israel-speak (or to be exact in Israel non-speak) "wait," "hold on," or "just a minute."

Another classic example of Israel non-speak is the famous Israeli "tsk." Apparently uttering the simple word "no" is considered to be too complicated, too time consuming, or perhaps just not macho enough, because in answer to a whole variety of questions, the average Israeli will simply make a sort of "tsk" sound. (A similar noise is made when loudly picking one's teeth.)

Here is a typical dialogue which, thanks to this uniquely Israeli trait, is transformed into a monologue:

"Have you eaten?"

"Tsk."

"Do you know what time it is?"

"Tsk."

"Would you like to make love all night long?"

"Tsk."

"Have you discovered the meaning of life?"

"Tsk."

Get the general idea? Tsk.

The Softer Side

Yet despite all the machismo, Israelis are much more family oriented "homebodies" than Americans or Europeans. Every work night finds the vast majority of them at home; and on Friday evenings, as well as every holiday, most either stay in or are out visiting their parents or relatives.

Israelis are not into eating out either. The restaurant culture which has engulfed the developed world has for the most part bypassed Israel. Home-cooked meals are almost always the rule, with the evening meal usually a light supper.

Israelis are perhaps the biggest salad eaters in the world, and one of the sure signs of spotting an Israeli is the way he or she will, twice a day at breakfast and dinner, prepare their salad by slowly, methodically and with exasperating patience cutting up tomatoes, cucumbers, and other ingredients into precise little squares.

Israeli social life also centers around the home. Not big for parties, the idea of a big night for the majority is either receiving guests at home, or visiting other homes for the traditional coffee, tea, and talk.

Along these lines, perhaps the biggest blow (at least for me) is that on the whole, Israelis do not drink. If the impression is beginning to form in your mind that many Israelis are somehow "square," you will encounter very little argument from this author. But square can be a positive attribute: if it also means very little alcohol, drugs, pretension, snobbery, class consciousness, and the other kinds of social games which are such a big part of being "in," then yes, Israelis are square. And they are proud of it.

But by far the biggest part of being an Israeli is the readiness and ability to deal with hardship and adversity. From the crowded morning bus, in which people automatically give up their seats to the elderly, to the threats of terrorism and war, a big step in "walking the Israeli walk" is learning how to keep your balance during the everyday crises which make up life here. This Israeli flair for walking the tightrope is a talent which has been learned through long, hard years of experience and suffering.

The American people have been criticized by many for somehow being "uneducated in human suffering." If such a thing can be said, then the opposite must hold true for the Israelis. Through their suffering, they have acquired a kind of wisdom, a wisdom which is the key to the secret of what it is to be an Israeli.

WELCOME TO THE CLUB

So there you have it. No matter where you were born, no matter how hard you think of yourself as culturally French, British, American, Russian, Ethiopian, Argentinean, South African or even Chinese, the inevitable telltale signs will begin to show after only a few months in the country.

There you'll be on the Sabbath day of rest – after buying enough food for a week rather than the lone one day off – with your

Welcome to the club! You're finally an Israeli!

sandaled feet up, the weekend papers on your lap, reading about Israeli politics and contentedly cracking sunflower seeds between your teeth. (You will discover that the sound made is similar to the Israeli "tsk".)

Nu, congratulations. You are an Israeli!

CULTURAL QUIZ

Are you really an Israeli? Can you pass for one? Get ready, because here comes the test.

SITUATION 1

Since politics dominates Israel, your first quiz will naturally be a political one, taken from recent Israeli history.

You've already read about the election crisis of 1990, which brought the Likud Party, along with a coalition of small extreme right-wing and ultraorthodox groups, to power. It all came down to the decision of two ultraorthodox spiritual leaders, one in Brooklyn and the other in Israel – a 92-year-old rabbi by the name of Rabbi Shach.

The speech in which Rabbi Shach was to announce his choice was broadcast live on Israel Television (and simultaneously translated into Hebrew because most of it was in Yiddish). As the nation was on the edge of its seat in anticipation, Rabbi Shach, instead of talking about whether he preferred Labor or Likud, or even about peace in general, devoted his entire speech to attacking the members of Israel's kibbutzim for eating pork.

The first question: according to his speech, how did Israelis know that the ultraorthodox would support the Likud?

A They could not have known, because pork-eating kibbutz members have nothing whatsoever to do with Israeli politics.

B They could not have known, because Labor and Likud are not religious parties, and many members of both parties eat pork.

C They could not have known, and the fact that both the Labor and Likud were not mentioned in the speech was evidence that Rabbi Shach would support neither party, because the ultraorthodox are traditionally anti-Zionist, don't believe in the state of Israel, and don't serve in the army.

D They most certainly knew, because the kibbutz movement has always been traditionally aligned with the Labor Party, and any attack on kibbutz members could automatically be interpreted as an attack on Labor – and conversely as implicit support for Likud.

Comments

A, **B**, and especially C are the most logical choices, but because logic has nothing whatsoever to do with Israeli politics, they are wrong. D, which makes the necessary pork-politics-power connection, is the correct, uniquely Israeli answer. Some religious leaders in Israel vote neither their conscience nor their pocketbooks, but their spareribs.

SITUATION 2

You are in a long line at the bank, standing behind a sign which says "wait here for your turn." After patiently biding your time, you have finally reached the head of the line. But just as you are about to cross the Rubicon and step up to one of the three tellers, a man hurries up, walks around the line as if it did not exist, and nonchalantly leans on the counter next to one of the clerks, waiting for her to finish with the current customer.

While you are still standing there watching all this with, as Richard Nixon used to say, "egg on your face," the clerk finishes with her previous customer and begins to do business with this man. What do you do?

A   Explode, make a scene, and start yelling at the man.

B   Adopt his method – go up to a counter, lean on it, and wait for the current customer to finish his or her business.

C   Go up to the man and calmly ask him to stand aside and get in line like everybody else.

D   Nothing.

Comments

There is no doubt that for Israelis, A is not only the acceptable but correct choice. I think the real answer depends on your blood pressure. If you are boiling inside, and your health will certainly be adversely affected if you don't do something, then either A or C (if you are less Israeli and more diplomatic) are the best choices. Why keep all that anger bottled up inside?

If on the other hand you find the whole thing amusing (which is highly unlikely if you have been waiting in line for half an hour), then D is the obvious choice. In my view, B is the most unworthy choice of all. If you are going to act like an Israeli, better act like an angry, righteous one than join the ranks of the sinners.

SITUATION 3

Looking for a good restaurant, you find one which is advertised as *halavi* (dairy). What can you expect to eat?

A Cows.

B Ice cream, milk shakes, and malts. In short, dairy products only.

C Everything.

D Everything, except meat or meat products. This can include fish (not seafood, of course, which isn't kosher), spaghetti (with a meatless meat sauce) or pizza (without sausage). With the dessert comes the true dairy part of the meal.

Comments

D is the correct, and kosher, answer.

SITUATION 4

You have been invited by friends to spend the weekend on their kibbutz. Traveling by bus or by car, you arrive at 3 p.m. on Friday, and seemingly find yourself in the middle of a ghost town. The place is dead quiet and there is absolutely no one around. What do you do?

A Turn around and go home.

B Try and locate the children's houses and nurseries, where you will certainly find someone who can direct you to your friends' house.

C Find your way to the children's houses, and play with the kids.

D Walk around the kibbutz until 4 p.m.

Comments

Certainly not A. Remember that between two and four in the afternoon on the kibbutz is the time of the sacrosanct two-hour nap. After getting up at 4:30 a.m. and spending half the night arguing kibbutz politics, it is only through this short snooze that the average kibbutznik has the strength to carry on.

B is only partly right. The children's houses are the natural choice to find some trace of human life on the kibbutz between two and four, because the kids are too filled with energy to sleep, and those assigned to watch over them could be the only adults awake at that hour.

But as far as having them direct you to your friends' house – that is the incorrect choice. There is no sin worse than waking up the kibbutznik during his or her daily nap. So that leaves either *C* or *D* as the correct answers. Remember that one of the Ten Commandments is "thou shalt not disturb thy kibbutznik's nap."

SITUATION 5

For one reason or another, you've decided to join the flock and become an Israeli citizen. Whether it's a prize or a punishment is one question. The more important point involves the price – induction into the Israeli Defense Force. What's the best way to prepare for the Israeli army?

A Pray.

B Start studying Hebrew as fast as you can. If you intend to volunteer for a combat unit, especially helpful will be learning the word "duck."

C Begin getting your body in shape – jogging, weightlifting, etc.

D Take some courses in meditation or other forms of relaxation and tension reduction therapy.

Comments

Praying can't hurt, but though relevant in the Holy Land, there are no guarantees that it'll always help. Studying Hebrew as fast as possible is of course recommended, but not essential. Most immigrants learn their Hebrew not before they enter the army, but during their time in it – and the process is an integral part of becoming a true Israeli. Physical conditioning is always healthy, but as hinted in the last suggestion, the main obstacle in coping with the army is not physical but mental. You can be in great shape physically and still find the IDF impossible if you don't learn how to relax and cope with the tension of being a soldier. And the most important attribute of all in successfully getting through your army service is a characteristic which cannot be learned – having a strong sense of humor. Those who don't know how to easily laugh often find themselves easily crying. But not to worry, the true answer to the question of how to prepare for the IDF is that there really is none. Like many experiences in life, just doing it will have to suffice.

SELECT BIBLIOGRAPHY

There have been so many books written about Israel, with every-body naturally taking a side, that it is hard to know just where to begin. As far as history is concerned, I have yet to come across one single general history of the country that even with a gigantic grain of salt could possibly be called objective. When the subject is Israel, everyone, whether they admit it or not, loses their objectivity.

So we may as well begin with two of the best of those who make no qualms whatsoever about taking sides: Israel's president at the time of writing, Chaim Herzog, is also a fine historian (and former head of IDF military intelligence). His book, *The Arab-Israeli Wars* (New York, Random House, 1982) makes for good reading. On the other side of the conflict is the famous Harvard professor Edward Said, who was among the select members of the Palestine Liberation Organization leadership in The Palestine National Council. His *Palestinian Lives* (New York, Pantheon Books, 1986) is extremely well written and worth a read.

The most entertaining way to read Israeli history could well be through biographies. Scores of them have been written on everyone from Yasser Arafat to Arik Sharon. Entertainment you will find; historical accuracy is another matter.

The best start could be with one of Israel's finest historians, Michael Bar-Zohar, whose famous official biography of the father of the country, *Ben-Gurion* (New York, Delacorte, 1978) is now regarded as a classic.

For more current history, I can recommend books by two of Israel's most respected journalists: Ze'ev Schiff and Ehud Ya'ari. They first collaborated on a very readable account of the war in Lebanon, *Israel's Lebanon War* (New York, Simon and Schuster,

1984) and later came together again with *Intifada* (New York, Simon and Schuster, 1990).

When one leaves the field of general history, it becomes much easier to find good books. For an excellent analysis of Israel from the political and economic point of view, I heartily recommend Daniel Shimshoni's *Israeli Democracy* (New York, Free Press, 1982).

On the ideological front, Israel's origins are best explored in a fine and highly readable anthology called *The Zionist Idea* (Arthur Hertzberg, editor, New York, Athenaeum, 1973).

A more contemporary look at the same question is offered by perhaps Israel's most impressive politician, Amnon Rubenstein. His book, *The Zionist Dream Revisited: Theodore Herzl to Gush Emunim* (New York, Schocken Books, 1984), is first-rate.

Some of the most enlightening books about Israel skip over the history and ideology and go straight to the people themselves. One of the best of these is Amos Elon's *The Israelis: Founders and Sons* (London, Weidenfeld and Nicolson, 1971).

A personal and highly emotional but nonetheless worthwhile pick is the extremely well-written *To Jerusalem and Back*, by Nobel Prize winner Saul Bellow (New York, Secker and Warburg, 1976).

The most personal look of all is given in another must, the now famous *Self-Portrait of a Hero: the Letters of Jonothan Netanyahu* (Benyamin Netanyahu, editor, New York, Ballantine Books, 1982).

However, the best way to discover Israel is through its fiction. Many Israeli authors, from Nobel Prize winning author S.Y. Agnon to the more recent David Grossman, have been translated into English.

Two of my personal favorites are A.B. Yehoshua's *The Lover* (New York, Dutton, 1985) and the best-selling novel of all time in Israel (in Hebrew that is), Amos Oz's *My Michael*, now out of print in English, but check your local library.

If you are looking for an explanation of just what the ultraorthodox are all about, perhaps the most readable and enjoyable way to learn can be found in Chaim Potok's wonderful fictional work *The Chosen* (New York, Simon and Schuster, 1967). The plot of the novel takes place in New York City, which, as far as the anti-Zionism of the ultraorthodox is concerned, I find rather appropriate.

And last but certainly not least, in how many countries in the world would the last book in a recommended reading list be the Holy Bible!

ACKNOWLEDGMENTS

I would like to thank the directors of Jerusalem's famous Haddassah Hospital, not for any lifesaving medical treatment, but for their splendid policy of bringing to Israel foreign doctors from the Third World to complete their training.

I was fortunate enough to befriend several of these outstanding young physicians, for whom Israel was about as familiar as the dark side of the moon. Seeing the country through their innocent and wondering eyes was a great help in writing this book.

First, the Mexicans: Dr. Luis Vidaurri, Dr. Eduardo Coronado, and Lourdes Coronado. From Haiti, thanks to my lifelong friend, Dr. Georges Beauvoir.

I am also grateful to Nomi Gaash for her patient help, as well as Jon and Ronit Epson, Iris Etzioni, Nadia Fradkova, Anna Siudut and the Zmora family: Hagai, Ruth, Anat, and Amir.

To the late Charles (Tava) Chadamunga of Zimbabwe – my eternal gratitude.

To Zvi Pantonovicz of Israel Radio, one of the country's finest and most unsung journalists, and to David Ehrlich of the *HaAretz* newspaper, my most heartfelt thanks.

On the academic side, my appreciation to Professor Paul Mendes-Flohr of the Hebrew University, and to professors Alan Jones, Joseph Wall, and Harold Kasimow of Grinnell College.

For *The Army in Israel*, my thanks to Israel Ben-Arieh, Danny Tapia, David Rosenthal, Alex Ben-Artzi, Mark Weiss, and Captain (Res) Mordechai Feldman.

For *Kibbutz*, my gratitude to the good people of Kibbutz Gshur: Yossi Egal, Eran Boren, Shlomit Levit, Alone Boren, Shi Egal, and Liore Nitzan.

And last but not least, to Jill Singer, Diane George, Elana Toledano, and Zohara Bar-Onne – my deepest appreciation for their unceasing moral support.

ABOUT THE AUTHOR

Dick Winter was born in the United States. In 1982, he became an Israeli citizen. During the Lebanon War, he did his regular army service as a sergeant in the paratroops. After his release from the IDF, he worked for Israel Radio as an editor and reporter, and later lived on Kibbutz Gshur on the Golan Heights. A writer, translator and freelance journalist, he now makes his home in Rehovot.

INDEX